Trompe L'Oeil Interiors

Trompe L'Oeil Interiors

Christopher Westall

NORTH LIGHT BOOKS
Cincinnati, Ohio

TO JAYNE, ADAM, AND HANNAH

A QUARTO BOOK

First published in North America in 2002
by North Light Books,
an imprint of F&W Publications, Inc.,
1507 Dana Avenue
Cincinnati, OH 45207

ISBN 1-58180-213-7

QUAR.MUTR

Conceived, designed, and produced by
Quarto Publishing plc
The Old Brewery
6 Blundell Street
London N7 9BH

Project editor Marie-Claire Muir
Senior art editor Elizabeth Healey
Designer Rod Teasdale
Photographers Paul Forrester & Colin Bowling
Copy editor Hazel Harrison
Illustrator Andrew Green
Proofreader Paula Reagan
Indexer Dorothy Frame
Art director Moira Clinch
Publisher Piers Spence

Manufactured by Universal Graphics (Pte) Ltd, Singapore
Printed by Star Standard (Pte) Ltd, Singapore

CONTENTS

INTRODUCTION

TROMPE L'OEIL IS A FRENCH TERM MEANING "TRICK THE EYE." A GOOD TROMPE L'OEIL MURAL CAN BLUR THE BOUNDARY BETWEEN FANTASY AND REALITY, MAKING THE VIEWER BELIEVE HE OR SHE IS LOOKING OUT ON A DELIGHTFUL LANDSCAPE, EVEN FROM THE CONFINES OF A WINDOWLESS ROOM.

LEAPING DOLPHINS
The famous leaping dolphins of Knossos in Crete (pictured on page 9) inspired this modern interpretation around an indoor swimming pool.

VILLAGE HARBOR

A picturesque village harbor has been re-created on the wall of a family home to serve as a fond reminder of a favorite vacation spot.

In a sense, trompe l'oeil murals can be seen as the ultimate form of escapism from the drab uniformity of modern life, but the creation of them is far from being an escapist occupation. Trompe l'oeil is a highly demanding branch of painting, and achieving success is extraordinarily satisfying.

In case you feel you are not equal to the task, let me tell you something about my own route into this profession. As a schoolboy I was in love with art, but my efforts were channeled into drawing, and I failed to see the appeal of painting. It was messy, could not be corrected with an eraser, and necessitated a lot of dull cleaning up afterwards. I could see no redeeming features at all.

Two events changed my perspective on this matter. The first was when my mother asked me to paint some popular cartoon characters on the walls of the children's department in our family shoe store. The second was when my art tutor informed me that I had to produce at least one painting in order to stand any chance of passing my examination.

And so I began to paint, and although I was never actually taught how to paint murals and trompe l'oeil, I gradually fumbled my way toward what interested me most, with the help of a few books not unlike this one. So I hope that this book will help you just as I have been helped in the past, and that it will provide a starting point for further research into the subject. If possible, seek out other examples of trompe l'oeil, both ancient and modern, so that you can analyze the tricks the artists have used to achieve their effects; looking at other people's work is an essential step toward developing your own visual language.

HOW TO USE THIS BOOK

This book is divided into four main sections. The first section deals with the practical aspects of mural painting, including general preparation and an overview of tools and materials. The second section deals with issues specific to trompe l'oeil painting and the art of illusion.

The Elements chapter serves two functions. Several of the elements demonstrated can be used on their own (for example, stone blocking and greenery), and with detailed instruction, all of them are easily manageable for the novice painter. They provide the opportunity to try out new skills before moving on to the Projects chapter, where the various elements are brought together in a series of full-scale trompe l'oeil murals, and are also a repertoire of "mix-and-match" features you can incorporate into your own designs.

These projects are only intended as a demonstration of my own methods, and an insight into the subjects that interest me personally. Try them out by all means, but don't feel you must copy them exactly. Always remember that good art comes from within, and each artist has different interests and ways of working. In time you will find your own artistic language, and if this book helps you to do this, it will have been a worthwhile enterprise. Finally, don't be discouraged if you make mistakes—I have made many, and each one has taught me something new. In the end, you learn to paint by doing it, so good luck with your endeavors.

Chris Westall

MURALS AND
THE ART OF ILLUSION

MURAL PAINTING IS ONE OF THE OLDEST ART
FORMS KNOWN TO HUMANKIND, AND THROUGHOUT HISTORY
MURALS HAVE BEEN CREATED TO PERFORM A VARIETY OF FUNCTIONS.
THEY HAVE RECORDED THE RITUALS OF DAILY LIFE AS WELL AS
IMPORTANT EVENTS FROM HISTORY AND LEGEND, THEY HAVE BEEN USED AS A
FORM OF COMMUNICATION AND PRAYER, AND, OF COURSE, THEY HAVE BEEN
EMPLOYED AS A PURELY DECORATIVE DEVICE.

The art of illusion is not confined to murals, although the mural form does facilitate the "trick" in trompe l'oeil art. Many painters of still life, both past and present, have played with the idea of trompe l'oeil, applying skill, and often humor, to "fool the eye"—legend has it that Rembrandt's students painted coins on the studio floor so that they could enjoy the sight of him bending down to pick them up.

HUMBLE BEGINNINGS

The first murals can be traced all the way back to early modern man, who sculpted recognizable art from rock, and painted and engraved onto cave walls with the crudest of instruments.

CAVE PAINTING

Cattle are gathered next to some huts, represented by white ovals. Animals, the favored subject of hunters, herdsmen, and breeders, seem to feature everywhere in early art.

Discovered examples date back to 38,000 B.C. in Europe, Africa, and Australia. During the late nineteenth century a series of caves was discovered in Spain and Southwestern France, the walls of which were covered with some of the most amazing paintings of animals ever seen—bulls, horses, and bison—painted with steady, flowing lines in earth colors directly onto the rough walls. These cave paintings, most notably in Lascaux in France and Altamira in Spain, were executed by simple hunting people between 18,000 and 15,000 B.C., and have been an inspiration to artists ever since they began to be seen and reproduced in the twentieth century.

ANCIENT CIVILIZATIONS

A more sophisticated tradition of wall painting grew up in the highly developed civilization of Ancient Egypt. This was a culture in which the afterlife had more importance than the transient cycle from birth to death, and it was the walls of tombs, not houses or palaces, that were decorated with paintings. Many of these are wonderfully decorative, and some depict birds and animals with great naturalism and a light-hearted touch. The painter's task was to ensure that the departed person was happy in the afterlife, surrounded by those things he had loved during his lifetime.

The Egyptians did not render perspective as we do, so the paintings lack the spatial element vital to trompe l'oeil murals, but they had a superb sense of design, and the works were executed with a bold, graphic simplicity that made them a powerful source of inspiration to the artists of the 1920s Art Deco movement.

Equally inspirational were the wall paintings produced by the seafaring Minoan nation on the island of Crete. At the height of their power, during the Bronze Age, the Minoans built great palaces, the best known being that of Knossos, which is decorated with marvelous paintings that give fascinating glimpses of the people's lifestyle. Favorite themes are dolphins, bullfights, and various forms of acrobatics.

These almost certainly influenced the later Classical Greek Civilization. In the art-oriented culture that produced the great sculptures of the Parthenon, it was certain that murals would have been painted in many of the houses of the well-to-do, but few have survived, although there are Roman murals that are believed to be copies of Greek originals.

In the Roman world, there are many well-documented examples of mural painting, with the best-known surviving examples being those at Pompeii, the town tragically buried in ash from an eruption of Vesuvius in A.D. 79. Although the laws of perspective were unknown, the Romans achieved a wonderful feeling of space and depth in their paintings, relying on careful observation to show them the way in which objects become smaller as they recede into the distance.

ROMAN FRESCO

This fresco, found in Pompeii, depicts an Amazon sitting near temple architecture.

MINOAN FRESCO

A fresco of fish and dolphins in the Queen's principal sitting room, Palace of Knossos, Crete, Greece. The border of the door was originally painted with rosettes, later with spirals. The door led to the King's quarters.

THE RENAISSANCE AND THE DISCOVERY OF PERSPECTIVE

After the fall of the Roman Empire, the painting of murals also went into decline. The murals of the Byzantine era were not embraced with the same vigor as they had been during the golden eras of the Greeks and Romans. Byzantine art was a stylized, religious art form distinguished by the unchanging laws of a Christian universe. The artists of the Renaissance showed a determination to move away from the religion-dominated Middle Ages and began to turn their attention to the plight of the individual man in society. It was a time when individual expression and worldly experience became two of the main themes of Renaissance art, giving birth to a new golden age with renewed interest in the works of the classical world of the Greeks and Romans.

In the early fifteenth century, the architect Filippo Brunelleschi "invented" perspective by formulating the mathematical laws that govern spatial relationships. He became famous almost overnight, and artists quickly saw how the new rules allowed them to create imaginary, believable space beyond the surface of the wall. The Florentine artist Masaccio was one of the first to put the ideas into practice, and the drama and realism of his masterly fresco cycle in the city's Brancacci Chapel make an incredible impact on the viewer. One of the most famous achievements of this era was Michelangelo's painting of the ceiling and end wall in the Sistine Chapel of the Vatican in Rome.

THE SISTINE CHAPEL (LEFT)

The ceiling of the Sistine Chapel is divided into sections depicting representations of the twelve apostles. Michelangelo achieved almost true trompe l'oeil effects through using boldly foreshortened forms.

VILLA FARNESINA (OPPOSITE)

This classical fresco was painted by Baldassare Peruzzi in 1515 in the Villa Farnesina in Rome. Peruzzi, who was also the architect of the villa, was an early pioneer in the use of perspective.

BAROQUE AND ROCOCO

From about 1600, the High Renaissance style that was characterized by Michelangelo developed into an even more theatrical one known as the Baroque, which relied heavily on illusion and extravagance for its effects. Artists such as Andrea Pozzo strove to blur the line between the real space and the illusion by painting architectural features that appear to be part of the actual architecture of the room.

The Rococo style, which emerged in the late seventeenth century, was a reaction to the grandeur and massiveness of the Baroque, and employed refined, elegant, and highly decorative natural forms, especially shells, which became one of the principal motifs. The term Rococo is derived from the French word *rocaille*, which means pebbles, and refers to the stones and shells used to decorate the interiors of caves.

Still life painting flourished during the seventeenth and eighteenth centuries, particularly in Holland, and often depicted a collection of objects that would remind the spectator of transience and mortality, for example, candles, flowers, hourglasses, and even skulls. There were also larger murals depicting interiors, usually kitchens, with food, flowers, animals, and cooks.

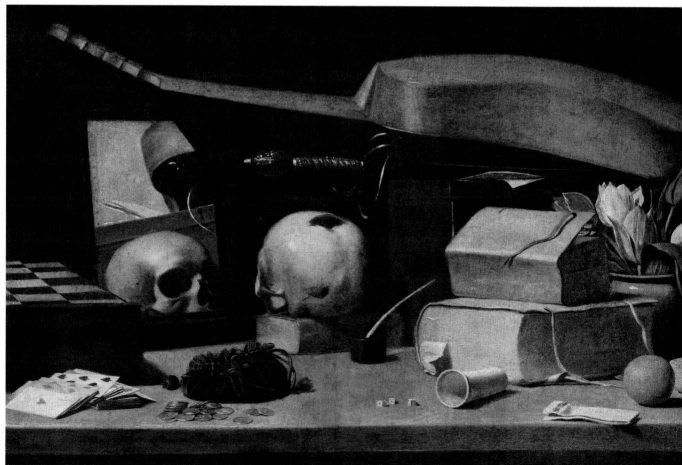

MEXICAN MURALISTS AND AMERICAN TROMPE L'OEIL

One of the reasons for the decline of the fresco tradition was that it could not withstand moisture, as this can cause both plaster and paint to crumble. Thus, the fresco was restricted largely to Italy, and was seldom used in Northern Europe. But it was the ideal technique for the dry climate of Mexico, where the last great murals were painted.

In 1921 President Obregón, a reformer and art lover, commissioned several artists to paint huge murals in public buildings. The purpose of these was to celebrate Mexican history and relate the events of the revolution, and the most famous of the artists was Diego Rivera. His works are quite unlike the great frescoes of the Renaissance era—his heroes were not saints and figures from myth but the common people, and he worked in a bold, colorful realistic style to portray their work, their hardships, and the contrasting lives of the rich and the poor.

When President Obregón was assassinated, the new regime could no longer tolerate the messages of these murals, and Rivera, together with two other muralists, Siqueiros and Orozco, were forced to flee to America. The three were then commissioned to paint large murals on buildings in California and New York as part of President Roosevelt's New Deal in the 1930s.

Trompe l'oeil still lifes became popular in nineteenth-century America, as the art-buying public admired the skill required to produce them. The American fascination of wealth was reflected in trompe l'oeil paintings of currency, which, even today, remains a characteristically American art form. Two artists, Nicholas Brookes and Otis Kaye, became so adept at producing fake money that a bill had to be passed in Congress prohibiting unofficial copies of bank notes.

Today, trompe l'oeil murals and paintings can be found in galleries beside fine art, as well as in public buildings, in parks and playgrounds, and in family homes around the globe.

ROCOCO MURAL (OPPOSITE, ABOVE)

This mural by Johann Bergl, with fruit and flowering trees, and a garden and townscape in the background, adorns the Garden Room of Schönbrunn Palace in Vienna, Austria. It was painted around 1770. Empress Maria Theresa used the room when the weather did not permit walks outside.

BAROQUE STILL LIFE (OPPOSITE, BELOW)

Still life painting, featuring wonderfully intricate and realistic portrayals of everyday objects, flourished in the seventeenth and eighteenth centuries. This example from the first half of the seventeenth century is by the French school of painters.

MEXICAN MURAL (RIGHT)

Mexico's dry climate makes it ideal for mural painting, and it was here that the last great murals were created. This mural in the Hospicio Cabañas in Guadalajara was painted by Jose Clemente Orozco between 1910 and 1920 to commemorate events in the Mexican revolution.

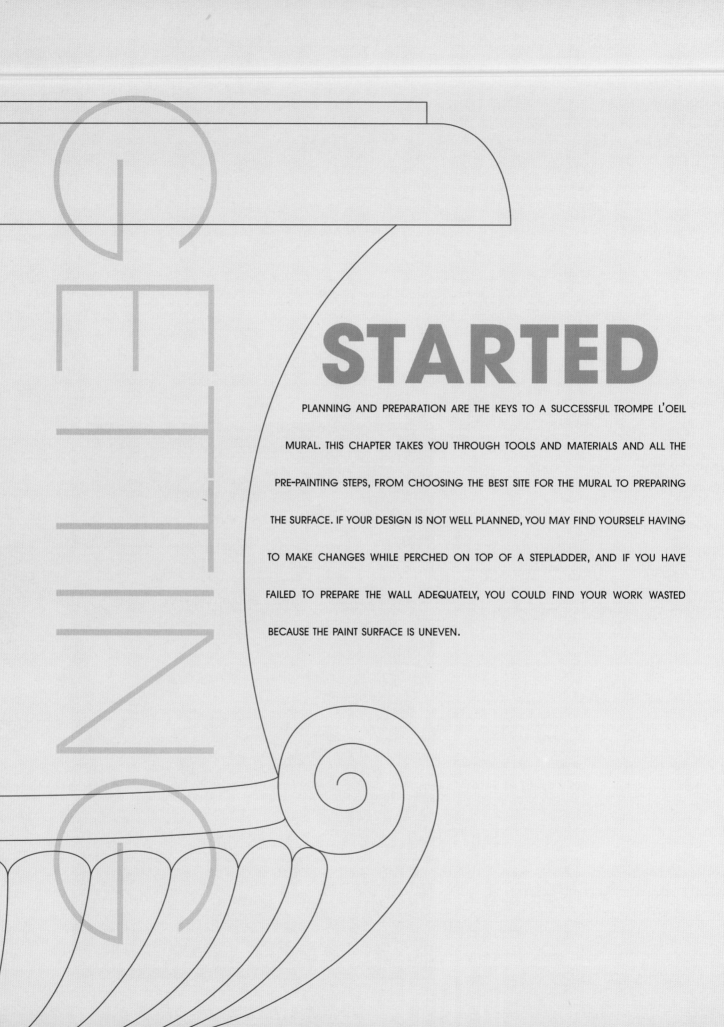

GETTING

STARTED

PLANNING AND PREPARATION ARE THE KEYS TO A SUCCESSFUL TROMPE L'OEIL

MURAL. THIS CHAPTER TAKES YOU THROUGH TOOLS AND MATERIALS AND ALL THE

PRE-PAINTING STEPS, FROM CHOOSING THE BEST SITE FOR THE MURAL TO PREPARING

THE SURFACE. IF YOUR DESIGN IS NOT WELL PLANNED, YOU MAY FIND YOURSELF HAVING

TO MAKE CHANGES WHILE PERCHED ON TOP OF A STEPLADDER, AND IF YOU HAVE

FAILED TO PREPARE THE WALL ADEQUATELY, YOU COULD FIND YOUR WORK WASTED

BECAUSE THE PAINT SURFACE IS UNEVEN.

FROM INSPIRATION
TO DESIGN

THE BEST STARTING POINT FOR FINDING INSPIRATION IS THE ROOM ITSELF. FIRST THINK ABOUT ITS CHARACTER AND FUNCTION. AN ENTRANCE HALL, FOR EXAMPLE, WOULD LEND ITSELF TO A FORMAL, PERHAPS CLASSICAL DESIGN TO MAKE A GRAND IMPRESSION ON GUESTS ENTERING THE HOUSE, WHILE A KITCHEN MIGHT BENEFIT FROM A SUNLIT FLOWER PIECE OR GARDEN SCENE TO TAKE THE MIND OFF THE MORE MUNDANE CULINARY CHORES. IN A SMALL ROOM, YOU COULD INCREASE THE PERCEIVED SPACE BY INVENTING A WINDOW VIEW WITH A LANDSCAPE STRETCHING FAR AWAY INTO THE DISTANCE.

CREATING A VIEW
One of nine classical panels painted around an ordinary modern sitting room. They create the illusion of being in a grand room surrounded by panoramic views of ancient Italy and Greece.

CREATING MOOD

Remember that even if you are painting a mural partly with the intent to impress others, your immediate family and you will be living with it from day to day, so it is vital to establish what kind of mood you want the painting to evoke. You might wish to enliven a rather gloomy sitting room, in which case a sunlit landscape could make a happy transformation, lifting your mood whenever you enter. A room that is attractive in itself, on the other hand, may require a more unobtrusive mural that blends in with the design of the room and its furnishings.

Bathrooms, where relaxation is usually the keynote, lend themselves to sky- or water-based designs, and if the room is large enough, you might even consider a more grandiose theme incorporating ancient Roman baths or ruined Greek temples with panoramic views.

FANTASIES AND FUN

A dining-room mural will be on public display from time to time, but a bedroom is less likely to be seen by non-family members. So here you could indulge in fun and fantasies, such as cherubs, drapery, sky ceilings, and moonlit balconies. Children's rooms provide an even greater outlet for this kind of creativity, and can be completely transformed into a fantasy world in which the child is surrounded with familiar friends from favorite stories, or perhaps with science-fiction scenes in popular films and videos.

PERSONAL TASTES

As in all branches of painting, your own interests will play a major role in your choice of design and the way in which you develop an idea. If you have a particular interest in flowers, for example, this will obviously be your starting point for collecting references and planning the design.

You might wish to re-create a favorite vacation spot or a landscape that appeals to you. This could range from huge vistas and seascapes to glimpses of a garden or tree seen through an open window. Think about the kind of landscape that has most impressed you—perhaps the magical colors of trees in the fall, the grandeur of a mountain range, the swirling patterns of moving water, or the quiet peace of a still lake at sunset or sunrise.

USING PHOTOGRAPHS

Photographs taken on vacation have been used as references for this African mural enveloping the walls and ceiling of a child's bedroom.

USING THE ROOM AS INSPIRATION

A witty trompe l'oeil painted onto the cupboards emphasizes the rustic charm of this country cottage kitchen.

COLLECTING REFERENCE

If you change the landscape you may also need to change the window—a louver window would not suit a chilly northern view—so collect architectural references as well as those for the landscape. Look through newspapers and magazines for any likely material, and keep a scrapbook, organizing it in such a way that you know where to find things. You might have separate sections for architectural features, as well as for different aspects of landscape—flowers, trees, grasses, water, distant hills, and so on.

Another excellent source of references is travel brochures. I have used photographs taken from these for the Western Scene project on page 106 and for the Tuscany Window project on page 116, and have over the years made full use of my local travel agents to find references for landscapes in numerous locations, including China, the Caribbean, Provence, and Venice, to name but a few. You are unlikely to find a picture that you can simply copy as it is—indeed this is not usually desirable. You may find an appealing piece of landscape in one picture, a detail of architecture in another, and perhaps a good tree in one more, and your end design will be a hybrid of all these different elements.

PLANNING YOUR DESIGN

Once you have both the idea and sufficient references, the next stage is to produce a concept design. It is a good idea to prepare your design in the context of a whole wall, particularly when

other architectural features are involved. Measure doors, windows, radiators, baseboards, light-switch and electrical-outlet plates, and so on. Then, reproduce them on a piece of sketch paper in a scaled-down version, keeping to the same proportions. This, known as the elevation, may take some time, so once you have finished it you may find it useful to make some photocopies in order to try out more than one design.

The camera as sketchbook

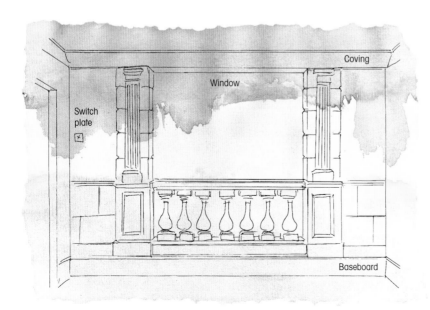

The camera is a useful tool for collecting visual reference material, but bear in mind that photographs can be disappointing unless the lighting is right. In general, the best times of the day to go out with your camera are early morning or evening, when the sun is low enough to cast the shadows that pick out form and detail. This is especially important for architectural features, because light and shadow help to explain the structures, which can otherwise be hard to understand.

SKETCHING YOUR DESIGN

Measure all the architectural features of the wall and reproduce them on a piece of sketch paper. Then draw your mural design on the paper, taking these features into account.

TIP If there are no doors or windows in the wall, it can be difficult to keep a sense of scale when planning the design. Sketching a rough human figure on the elevation may help.

Coving

Window

Switch plate

Baseboard

THE CONCEPT SKETCH

Concept sketches are essential to me, as I use them to show my clients how their mural will look. If they have any doubts, they can tell me at this point rather than waiting until I am halfway through painting. But even for the non-professional, the sketch is important, as it will enable you to see roughly how your idea will work and whether it will have the desired effect. It is much easier to make corrections and alterations on paper than it is to rework the painting itself if things seem to be going wrong.

How you go about making the sketch is largely up to you; you can use any materials you are happy with. I begin by mapping out the design with a graphite pencil, then build up the main areas of color with colored pencils, and finally define the design detail using a fine ink pen. My sketches are basically rough guides as to composition and color, but if you wish, you can produce a more intricate design and then scale it up onto the wall (see pages 32–33.)

CHINESE GARDEN

After assessing the sketch, I decided to move the pagoda farther into the distance and introduce more green landscape in the middleground.

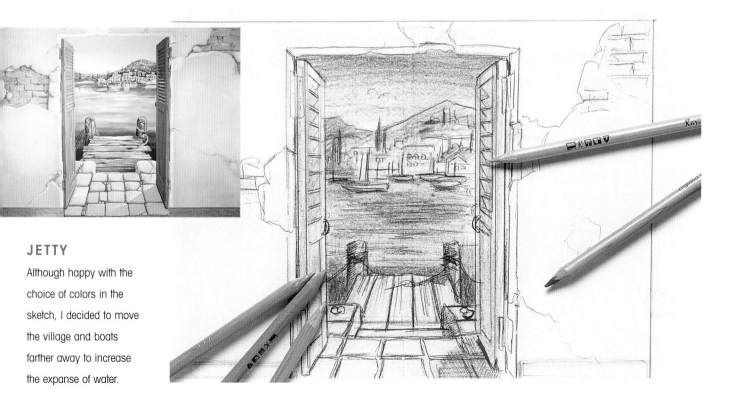

JETTY

Although happy with the choice of colors in the sketch, I decided to move the village and boats farther away to increase the expanse of water.

CHOOSING A SITE

As for buying property, one of the most vital considerations for a successful trompe l'oeil—perhaps the most important of all—is location.

THE VIEWPOINT

If your mural is to achieve maximum impact and to be fully appreciated, it must be placed where it can be seen from the best possible vantage point.

Trompe l'oeil murals like the Stone Archway & Classical Garden (page 96), Western Scene (page 106), and Tuscany Window (page 116) all depend heavily on depth and the use of perspective. They invite you to look beyond the trompe l'oeil "frame"—whether it is a window, archway, or door—to features in the distance. If this type of mural were painted on the side wall of a narrow hallway, the viewer would be unable to stand far enough away from the painting to benefit from the full effect, and however meticulously painted, the trompe l'oeil would lose its effect. Generally speaking, if the *trompe* involves distance, it should ideally be viewed from a distance.

Murals that have a strong emphasis on perspective will also appear distorted if they are not viewed from the angle at which they are painted—usually face on. It can be quite effective to paint such scenes so that the best vantage point is the entrance to a room (which would usually position it on the wall opposite the entrance). This has the additional advantage of providing an element of surprise, and thus increasing the impact of the trompe l'oeil.

Alternatively, choose a place where the mural can be viewed from a static position, by those seated at a dining-room table or on a sofa, for example. In this case you would need to consider the eye level, especially in the case of landscapes. For a trompe l'oeil landscape to be effective, the horizon needs to be more or less at eye level. So if it is to be most commonly viewed from a sitting position, you will need to adjust the vanishing point of your mural accordingly (see pages 36–39 for more information on perspective).

A "shallow" trompe l'oeil, one that does not rely heavily on perspective, can be effective just about anywhere. The most obvious example is stone blocking. Its "depth" is minimal, and it would still be effective even in a narrow hallway, viewed from an angle. Ivy creeping up the wall, playing cards on a table, or a postcard "pinned" on a kitchen cupboard are other examples.

Although the majority of murals are painted inside houses, they don't have to be. Outdoor courtyards and garden fences are perfect for trompe l'oeils—perhaps some colorful foliage, a bird, or even a "pet" dog or cat. I once painted a small trompe l'oeil of a perched wood pigeon on the face of a chimney stack.

PANORAMIC SEA VIEWS

A pair of trompe l'oeil binoculars have been provided to admire the painted sea views. The grid pattern of the painted windows echoes the mirrors in the corner of the room, while the mirrors themselves reflect the mural to make it a complete panorama when viewed from the entrance opposite.

SIZE AND SCALE

Another very important consideration when planning a mural is its relationship to the size and proportions of the room in which it is to be painted. Remember that any trompe l'oeil features painted "within" the room, for example, windows, pillars, ivy, or a pot plant, need to be painted at life size. Generally, a trompe l'oeil gains greater credibility the farther the viewer can stand

back from it. So a large mural, or at least a mural with large features, will require a room of generous proportions.

Modern housing seldom provides large amounts of space, so the projects in this book have been tailored to suit rooms of normal size; they are all relatively small-scale and could be painted in almost any home. Tiny areas can be more challenging, but you do not need to avoid them altogether. I have painted many murals on bathroom walls, one being the interior of an E-Type Jaguar. The client liked the idea of seeing the dashboard while sitting on the toilet, and although the overall effect was somewhat overpowering, I managed to get away with it since the room was only used for short periods of time.

ARCHITECTURAL FEATURES

When you have decided on a site, look around the room and see whether there are any architectural features that might be used to the advantage of the mural. A doorway, for example, could be incorporated into the scheme, with a pediment painted above. Floor tiles could be painted so that they extend into the imaginary space of the mural, and even chair rails and wall moldings can be utilized in a design.

Pipes, switch plates, and radiators are usually a nuisance, as continuing the design over them may just draw more attention to them. In most cases, the best course is simply to paint them in a blending color to play down their intrusiveness.

THEATRICAL DRAPERY

A shimmering red curtain painted across a door helps to create a theatrical feeling. It is also a good way to incorporate a mural in a room without any spare wall space.

INTERGALACTIC ODYSSEY

A row of drab closets have been transformed into a window into outer space in this young boy's room. The moldings on the closets make ideal window frames, while the panels are perfect for the view of space.

PREPARING THE SURFACE

Unless walls are in exceptionally good condition, they will need preparing before you begin your mural. This may seem a tedious chore, but it is an important stage because without a good foundation your mural could deteriorate, wasting all your hard work.

PREPARING THE WORKING AREA

Start by clearing as much space as possible in the area you are to be working and cover the floor with drop cloths (or old sheets provided they have no holes), fixing them to the baseboards with masking tape for complete protection. Also stick tape along the top edge of the baseboard to catch any paint drips.

Dirt and grime can build up on walls over a period of time, so unless the room has been newly decorated, walls painted with latex (emulsion) paint should be cleaned with a strong cleanser. Wear rubber gloves when using powerful cleansing products, and rinse the surface thoroughly with clean water afterwards.

Newly plastered walls require little preparation, but they should be sanded when completely dry and then coated with a new-plaster sealer.

OIL-PAINTED AND PAPERED SURFACES

Rub down old oil-painted surfaces with sandpaper to provide a key for the subsequent priming. A new coat of oil-based paint, however, will need to be removed, which you can do with a blowdryer (or hair dryer) and a wallpaper scraper. Try not to leave any odd patches, as you will find that these take longer to dry when you prime the wall.

Matte wallpaper, if it is smooth and in good condition, is perfectly suitable to be primed ready for a mural, but textured or shiny wallpaper will have to be removed, taking care not to damage the surface of the wall. However, it is usually easy to repair walls if you do spoil small areas, or uncover previously hidden cracks.

TIPS

• Salty deposits appearing through the wall can point to damp problems, especially in the case of an exterior wall. Remove the deposits with a stiff brush and then prime the wall with an alkali-resistant stabilizing solution.

• Mold on the walls may simply be caused by condensation, usually indicating insufficient ventilation. If you cannot install a wall ventilator in the room, a de-humidifier could be the answer. Mold can be removed with a water and bleach solution or a specially formulated mold cleaner.

FILLING CRACKS

First scrape and brush out any bits of dust and plaster from the cracks and chips with a screwdriver and then a paintbrush. Repair them with good-quality, all-purpose spackling paste (decorator's filler)—I prefer the powder variety that you mix yourself, as I find it easier to sand down than the ready-mixed version. Fill large cracks with a trowel, and smaller ones with a putty knife.

Allow the paste to dry out thoroughly, and repeat if necessary—the paste usually contracts as it dries—then sand down both the paste and the surrounding area of wall. You may wish to wear a protective facemask to avoid inhaling any of the fine dust. Make sure to clear up all the dust with a vacuum cleaner before you start painting or it will stick to the priming coat.

USING CRACKS IN THE DESIGN (OPPOSITE)

Cracks and dents occur naturally in sandstone and, of course, crumbling walls. If you want to use these effects across an entire wall, you can save yourself the effort of filling in existing blemishes, as they can be left to enhance the effect.

PRIMING THE SURFACE

Before you begin to prime the wall, mask out any features such as light fittings, switch plates, door architraves, and so on if you are painting up to them. If the masking tape is applied to an already painted surface, use a low-tack one so that it doesn't pull off any paint when you remove it. If you can't buy low-tack tape, stick pieces of the ordinary tape to your sleeve or your hand and then remove it—this makes it less sticky.

PRIMING

Water down the first coat slightly and build up at least two or three coats.

PREPARING PANELS

You may prefer to paint on a panel rather than directly onto the wall, in which case you could use MDF (medium-density fiberboard), plywood, hardboard, or chipboard. The panel can then by attached to the wall in the desired location. MDF comes in a variety of thicknesses, and an exterior version is also available, a good choice for a bathroom for example.

Because MDF has a smooth finish, you will need to sand it before priming to provide a key for the paint (when doing this, wear a mask to prevent inhaling the dust, which can be harmful).

The priming coat, or base coat, should be matte latex (emulsion) in any color that suits the mural—but obviously not too dark. The first coat should be slightly watered down, especially on a new plaster wall. The paint can be applied with a roller (but be careful not to overload it if using watered-down paint), a large decorator's brush, or a paint pad. Use a smaller brush to paint up to and around any wall fittings etc. Although these will have been masked, paint can creep in underneath the tape if applied too liberally.

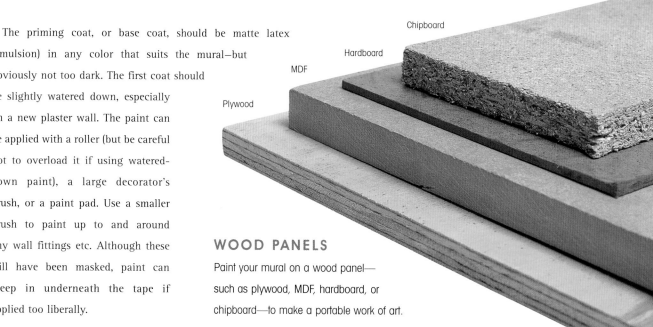

Chipboard

Hardboard

MDF

Plywood

WOOD PANELS

Paint your mural on a wood panel— such as plywood, MDF, hardboard, or chipboard—to make a portable work of art.

TIPS

• To protect the floor, you could lay down sheets of hardboard instead of drop cloths, joining them together with masking tape. This is more expensive, but can be worthwhile. It gives you a sounder surface to stand on, and is safer, as cloths quickly become bunched up, and it is all too easy to trip over them. Hardboard also offers more protection if there is any paint spillage.

• When using larger-sized panels that will not be fixed flush to the wall, it is a wise precaution to prime the backs of the panels and/or to fix strips of wood to them to prevent warping. This applies especially to hardboard panels.

• The corners of MDF panels are vulnerable to damage if you drop them, so sand them down to curve the edges slightly.

GOTHIC WINDOW

This shaped MDF panel shows a Gothic window looking out over a classical landscape. Panels such as this can be moved to new locations.

The board can then be primed using either acrylic primer or standard latex (emulsion) paint and a roller, decorator's brush, or paint pad. Water down the first coat slightly and build up two or three good coats, leaving each one to dry and lightly sanding between coats.

Hardboard is an inexpensive alternative, but is less strong than MDF and is prone to warping. This also must be sanded before priming, as the surface is too shiny to hold the paint. Plywood, made from either three or five thin sheets of wood glued together—described as three-ply and five-ply—is relatively strong, but the edges are prone to split so will need to be protected with a frame or painted with a sealer primer. Chipboard, made from compressed wood chips in resin, is very heavy and thus hard to manipulate, and the edges tend to wear easily. Both chipboard and plywood have a rather obtrusive surface texture, and will need several coats of priming to provide a smooth surface.

TOOLS AND MATERIALS

You will not need an extensive range of materials for mural painting, but it is important that both paints and brushes are of good quality, and that paints especially are chosen with the position of the mural in mind. For most of my murals I use a combination of ordinary household latex (emulsion) paint and artist's acrylics, but in a bathroom, where the mural will be exposed to high levels of humidity, I would recommend an exterior latex (emulsion) or one containing fungicides. Artist's acrylics can withstand changes in moisture levels, but household paint can sometimes flake or attract mold growth.

PAINTS

Both latex (emulsion) paints and artist's acrylics are water based, so they can be easily mixed together, and both are durable and quick to dry. The latter quality is a great advantage, as most murals are built up gradually in layers. If you were to use slow-drying paints such as oils, a lot of time would be wasted waiting for each layer to dry. Oil paints also have a strong odor, as do the solvents used to thin the paints and clean brushes, to which some people are allergic. Water-based paints have very little odor—acrylics have none at all—and soap and water are all you need to clean your brushes and hands after work.

ARTIST'S ACRYLICS What makes these paints—and latex (emulsion)—different from others is that the pigments are bound with polymer resin rather than with natural oils or gums, and it is this resin that makes them so tough. Once dry, the resin forms a kind of plastic coating that cannot be removed and is not susceptible to damage. And, equally important, the colors do not yellow with age as oil paints do.

Acrylics are also wonderfully versatile, which is the main reason for their increasing popularity with artists. When thinned with water, they can be used almost like watercolor, in thin washes, but by using them at tube consistency you can build up textured layers of paint that look very similar to oil colors.

Although the fast drying time of acrylics is usually a bonus, you may need to extend it for certain paint effects such as marbling and graining, in which case you can add a specially formulated medium called acrylic retarder.

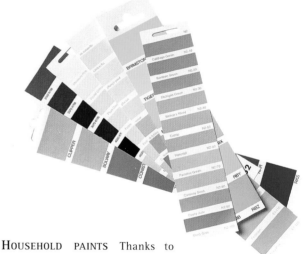

HOUSEHOLD PAINTS Thanks to ever-advancing technology, it is now possible to obtain almost any color of latex (emulsion) you want. This is especially useful when you need large quantities, perhaps for a sky. If you run out, all you have to do is buy another can rather than trying to mix up exactly the same color again—which is almost impossible, because the colors tends to dry slightly darker than they appear when wet (this is also the case with artist's acrylics). When you buy these paints, look carefully at the label so that you don't accidentally purchase one of the satin-finish varieties. These can look good on walls, but are not suitable for trompe l'oeil work because the sheen will reflect the light and, thus, ruin the illusion.

help you. If you are using a new product, test it out on an area other than the mural to see whether it gives off a sheen when dry; be wary, as sheen can ruin the trompe l'oeil effect.

The varnish can be applied with a varnishing brush, but these tend to leave brushmarks, so to produce an even surface, I recommend a paint pad. Work all over the surface very much as a window cleaner does with a squeegee, but make sure that the pad is not overloaded, as this could cause drips and runs.

Apart from the convenience of using household paint, there is also a good economic reason. You will always be using more white than any other color, as all colors lighter than a mid tone will be mixed with white. Using large quantities of acrylic white would be expensive, but you can buy a large can of household paint for very little. The same applies to any other colors—if you start with a can of household paint in, say, blue or beige, you can amend it by mixing in acrylics to achieve the desired hue.

BRUSHES

For covering large areas you will need paintbrushes in various sizes. The most important rule when buying these is to avoid the cheap ones—they may save you money in the short term but this is a false economy, as you will spend more time picking hairs out of the paint than you will on actually painting. The brushes will last a long time if you look after them properly.

VARNISH

Although acrylic paints are tough, murals will be exposed to air for a long time, so they do need to be protected with at least two coats of varnish. This also helps to unify the surface. When you use acrylics you may notice that some areas dry with a matte surface while others have a slight sheen. These surface differences could detract from the overall effect, but varnishing will even them out.

There are a great many types of varnish on the market, but some, such as polyurethane and various oil varnishes, are intended for wood, and they yellow with age. You need a matte-surfaced colorless acrylic varnish formulated for the purpose—these appear white in the bottle or can but dry perfectly clear and will not discolor. I use a matte acrylic varnish from a specialist paint manufacturer, but most good art suppliers will be able to

ARTIST'S BRUSHES These come in a wide range of sizes, and are made of various materials, both natural and synthetic. The most expensive brushes are sable, used mainly by watercolor painters. You might find one small sable useful for fine detailing, but you are unlikely to require more. The traditional oil painter's brush is made of hog hair, but there are many good synthetic alternatives, which I personally prefer for acrylic work. These alternatives are flexible, pleasant to use, and relatively inexpensive. But ultimately, the choice of brushes is a personal one, and you will only find out which ones you prefer by trying them out.

Synthetic brushes are sold in two main shapes: flat and round (pointed), and some ranges also offer a third shape, called a filbert, which has a rounded but not pointed top. Flats are ideal for blending and graduating color, as in a sky, and also for stippling in details for foliage effects, while round brushes are the best for detailing. These do not last as well as flats, as the tips can become frayed unless extra care is taken.

DECORATOR'S BRUSHES These are useful for priming the surface before painting. They can also be used to cover large areas with paint quickly and to apply color washes.

VARNISHING BRUSHES Like the artist's brushes, these are available in many sizes and in both round and flat varieties. I have used a flat hog-hair varnish brush in some of the projects for general blocking in and blending in of colors over larger areas where a flat synthetic brush would be inadequate.

ROLLERS AND PAINT PADS Rollers are useful for painting large areas of a single color, when laying a base color for a mural, for example. The best type to use is a short-pile roller, as this gives a flatter and more even surface than the shaggier ones. Rollers are usually sold with a paint tray, which provides a well for the paint and a flat surface onto which you can remove any excess. Paint pads, which consist of a short pile on a sponge backing, are less messy than rollers. Like the latter, they come in a variety of sizes, and can be ideal for cutting into tight corners.

TIPS

• Before using a new brush for the first time, gently wash it in warm running water, rubbing the bristles with your fingers to remove any excess or stray bristles. This will ensure that none come loose and end up in your mural.

• Remember that acrylic cannot be removed once dry, so always keep brushes moist while working. Do not leave them upside down in a jar of water, as this may bend the bristles. Instead, place them on their sides in a shallow bowl of water.

• After a working session, wash brushes well with warm soapy water.

• If the bristles on round artist's brushes become distorted, clean the brush in warm soapy water, dry it, then hold the bristles in the steam of a boiling kettle for a few seconds. Then scrape some soap from a soap bar and use it to re-shape the bristles. Leave to set.

• If you accidentally let the paint dry on a brush, leave it to soak in denatured alcohol (methylated spirits) for about half an hour. Then, gently work the paint out of the bristles with your fingers. The brush will not be as good as new, but it may be usable.

• Store your artist's brushes in a container with the bristles pointing up. Try not to overcrowd the container, as the brushes should not rest on each other. Larger paintbrushes usually have a hole in the end of the handle so they can be hung from a hook with the bristles down. This helps to drain out the water used for washing.

EQUIPMENT FOR PREPARATION AND PAINTING

You will need various pieces of equipment for the pre-painting stages, when you are getting the wall ready for the mural. If you do your own decorating, you will already own at least some of these.

DROP CLOTHS (DUST COVERS) These are used to protect all vulnerable areas like carpets and furniture, and are available from some home improvement stores. You can also use old sheets or plastic sheeting, but the latter is easy to slip on.

STRONG CLEANSER (SUGAR SOAP) You can purchase powerful cleansing products from home improvement and paint stores that will remove any grease and dirt from the wall.

SPACKLING PASTE (DECORATOR'S FILLER) AND PUTTY KNIFE Used to repair cracks in the wall surface prior to rubbing down.

SANDPAPER AND/OR SANDING BLOCK Used to remove any flaking paint, to rub down spackling paste, and to provide a key for the subsequent paint layer. If possible, stock various grits of sandpaper, from coarse to fine, for different tasks.

STEPLADDER You will need one for both the preparation stages and for the mural itself, to make sure you can reach all the areas comfortably. A three- or four-step lightweight aluminum ladder will be suitable for most murals, though for larger ones you may need a portable scaffolding tower. You would have to rent this from a scaffolding company—if possible, get them to assemble it and show you the correct and safe way to use and move it.

LEVEL This provides the most convenient and reliable means of checking and drawing in your horizontals and verticals. Ideally you should have two sizes: a standard one and a smaller carpenter's level, so that the larger level can also double up as a straightedge.

STEEL TAPE MEASURE Use one that shows both imperial and metric measurements.

STEEL OR PLASTIC RULER For making accurate measurements on the wall and to use as a straightedge.

CHARCOAL AND GRAPHITE PENCILS Use charcoal pencils for general sketching, and graphite pencils for accurate markings, but bear in mind that graphite marks are harder to remove than charcoal ones.

SEMI-TRANSPARENT TRANSFER PAPER For planning out images and templates and transferring them onto the wall. Ordinary kitchen wax paper can be used as an alternative.

CALCULATOR Invaluable for scaling up templates (see page 32) and preparing the wall for stone blocking (see page 46).

STRING To help with establishing the correct perspective lines. Colored string is best, as it is more visible than white string.

PLASTIC CUPS (POTS) AND SPOONS For mixing and holding paint. Small plastic cups and larger plastic containers can be bought in food stores. Plastic spoons are also widely available—use these to spoon out small quantities of paint from latex (emulsion) cans.

PERMANENT MARKER PEN For labeling the plastic cups (pots) to enable you to find the right color when you need to use it again.

MASKING TAPE To protect from paint such areas as light switches and electrical sockets. Can also be used to mask off areas within the mural to create crisp, straight edges. Masking tape is available in various widths, but 1 inch (2.5cm) will be sufficient for most jobs. Buy low-tack if possible.

ILLUSIONS

IT IS NOW TIME TO SCALE UP YOUR DESIGN AND TRANSFER IT TO THE WALL. CORRECT PERSPECTIVE IS ESSENTIAL FOR SUCCESSFUL TROMPE L'OEILS, AND A GRASP OF THE SIMPLE RULES WILL ENABLE YOU TO MAKE YOUR MURALS A CONVINCING A DEPICTION OF THE REAL WORLD. BEFORE THE ACTUAL PAINTING BEGINS, YOU SHOULD HAVE A BASIC APPRECIATION OF THE COLOR THEORY AND UNDERSTAND THE WAY LIGHT AND SHADOW DEFINE FORM.

FROM DRAWING
TO PAINTING

THE GRID METHOD

Draw a grid over the template, then draw a larger grid at the size you want the template to be scaled up to. Make sure the grids are divided into the same number of blocks and are of the same proportions, then copy the contents of each block from the template onto the larger grid.

THE MAJORITY OF THE PROJECTS IN THE BOOK INCLUDE TEMPLATES, MANY OF WHICH WILL NEED TO BE ENLARGED, OR SCALED UP. BECAUSE THE TEMPLATES ARE OVERLAID WITH TEXT, YOU WILL FIND IT EASIEST TO START BY TRACING THEM ONTO A SHEET OF CLEAN TRACING OR TRANSFER PAPER.

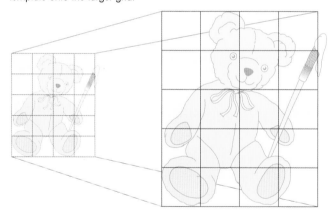

SQUARING UP

Also known as the grid method, this is a simple technique, if a little time-consuming. First draw a grid over the traced image, and then draw another, larger grid with the same number of squares on a commensurately larger piece of transfer paper—you can join two or more sheets together if necessary. You will need to establish the size you want the image to be before you start. For example you may want it one-and-a-half or twice the size of the template, in which case the squares on the transfer paper must be this amount larger. When you have drawn both grids, transfer the image carefully from one to the other. If you wish to scale down, as you might in the case of some small landscape feature, the second grid must obviously be smaller than the first.

CALCULATING MEASUREMENTS

Scaling up height and width measurements is a simple process. Measure the height of the template (y) and the height you wish to scale it to (x). Dividing x by y gives another figure, z. When you want to scale up other measurements from the template, simply multiply them by z. For example, the height of the baluster template on page 54 is 15 inches (38cm). If you want the height to be 25 inches (63.5cm), the calculation would be: 25 (x) ÷ 15 (y) = 1.6 (z).

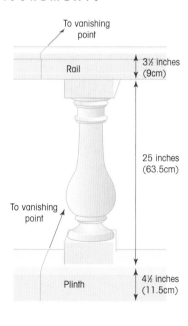

To vanishing point

3½ inches (9cm)

Rail

25 inches (63.5cm)

To vanishing point

Plinth

4½ inches (11.5cm)

TIP For symmetrical designs such as the baluster template on page 54 you only need to scale up half the image. When this is complete, simply fold the paper down the middle and trace the other half.

USING A CALCULATOR

A can be used to work out the relative heights of the rail and plinth for balustrading. The actual heights of this particular balustrading are marked on the diagram (opposite, right). Remember that if the balustrade is set back into the mural you will have to adjust the sizes accordingly, using this technique in conjunction with the Diminishing size method, page 38.

USING A SCANNER

This accurate method of scaling up allows you to manipulate images as well as store them for future use. Large templates can be printed on several sheets of paper, which can then be taped together.

PROJECTION METHOD

Drawing your image on an acetate sheet, projecting it onto the wall using an overhead projector, and drawing over it may seem a foolproof method, but in fact there are a good many pitfalls. Unless the image is projected squarely onto the wall, which can be difficult, there will be distortions. You can only alter the size of the image by moving the projector nearer or farther from the wall, so in a small room you may not be able to enlarge to the size you want. The lighting needs to be subdued so that you can see the image clearly, but this makes drawing difficult, added to which your hand and body will be casting shadows, so you will have to keep turning off the projector in order to check your progress. A better alternative might be to project the image onto transfer paper first and then transfer it to the wall as described on pages 34–35.

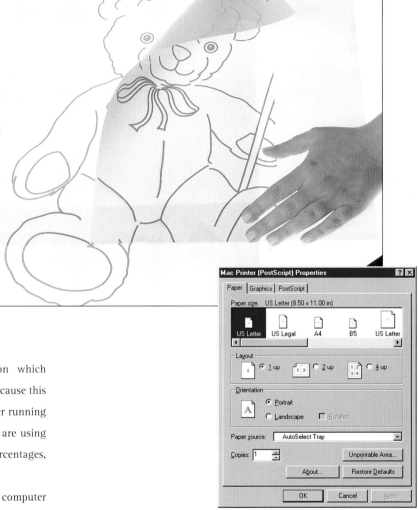

PHOTOCOPIERS AND SCANNERS

Most people now have access to photocopiers, on which enlargements can be made by using percentages, and because this is a relatively quick and easy process you could consider running off a few copies of varying sizes for future use. If you are using a public copier, and are not sure how to work out the percentages, there is usually someone on hand to help.

For those with the know-how and equipment, a computer scanner provides an even better method. The scanned images can be manipulated in an image package, of which there are several on the market, sized accordingly, and then printed. The image will normally need to be larger than standard-size printing paper, but most image manipulation packages allow for printing on more than one sheet of paper, which can then be taped together to form the larger image.

TRANSFERRING IMAGES

Once you have scaled up your templates or photographic reference, you will need to transfer the designs onto the wall. The basic techniques are simple. Indeed many people will remember the process of scribbling on the back of a piece of tracing paper from their school days.

SEMI-TRANSPARENT TRANSFER PAPER

If your design has been planned out on transfer paper, turn it over and draw a thick pencil line over all the outlines, using either a charcoal pencil or a soft graphite pencil such as a 6B.

Turn the paper to the right side and position it on the wall, taping it in place with low-tack masking tape. Once the paper is in place, stand back to check whether you are happy with the position. Then, using an HB pencil, draw over the outlines to leave an imprint on the wall.

TIP Disasters can happen, such as a gust of wind blowing the paper off the wall before you have completed the drawing. Or you may need to remove it temporarily for some reason. To ensure that you can re-align the paper in the exact position if necessary, draw short double lines at the edges, crossing over and marking the wall.

WAX PAPER

Ordinary kitchen wax paper is a good alternative if you do not have any transfer paper.

OPAQUE PAPER

If your design is on ordinary photocopier or printer paper it will still be possible to draw over the outlines on the reverse, but you will need to hold the paper up against a window so that the light shines through it. You should then be able to see the outlines clearly. Alternatively, you could use graphite or carbon paper to transfer the image. Tape the carbon paper to the wall first, and then place the design on top and trace it onto the wall.

There is one thing to watch out for when using non-transparent paper, which is that you cannot see through it when it is on the wall. So before sticking it on, draw vertical and horizontal lines from edge to edge of the design, and then longer and wider verticals and horizontals on the wall. All you then need to do is to match the lines so that the image is correctly aligned.

WINDOW LIGHTBOX

If you have used opaque paper, tape the image to a window so that it becomes semi-transparent and you can then draw over the outlines on the reverse of the paper.

TRACING SYMMETRICAL AND GEOMETRIC DESIGNS

In the Stone Urn project on page 90, a template of only half of the urn was used, and this was then flipped over to trace the other side onto the wall. When you do this, you must first draw an accurate center, a vertical line on the image, establish exactly where it is to placed, and draw another vertical on the wall. It is also helpful to establish a horizontal line on both the image and the wall, as this makes it easier to re-align the image for tracing the other side.

If the image you are transferring contains horizontal and vertical lines, it is important to make sure they are true. For example, if the temple template provided for the Stone Archway & Classical Garden project on page 96 were transferred onto the wall even at a very slight angle, the effect would be very jarring indeed. When drawing vertical and horizontal lines on the wall, hold the pencil against a level to ensure that the lines are true.

PERSPECTIVE

Perspective is the means by which we describe spatial relationships. Although you do not need to study perspective in detail, a grasp of the basic rules is vital for creating the illusion of three dimensions on a two-dimensional surface. The main and most important rule is that of diminishing size—that is, the way in which objects appear smaller the farther away they are.

ONE-POINT PERSPECTIVE

Because things become smaller as they recede, the spaces between them also diminish in size. This leads to the second basic rule, which is that receding parallel lines appear to converge gradually, and will, if uninterrupted, eventually meet. This simple system, known as one-point, or linear, perspective, is all you will need to achieve the effects shown in the elements and projects in the later chapters of the book. It involves three main elements.

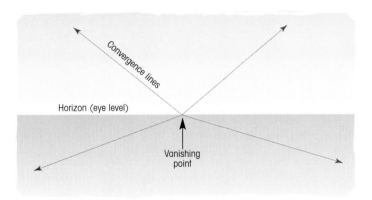

HORIZON LINE The point at which the parallel lines meet is located on an imaginary line called the horizon line. The word horizon is often used loosely to describe the boundary between land and sky, but it has a much more specific meaning in perspective—it is simply the level of your own eyes, and is also known as "eye level." Obviously, this line moves with your movement, being higher if you are standing than if you are sitting. This is why it is important to bear the eye level in mind when planning a mural; if viewers are likely to be seated when they look at it, too high an eye level could be distracting. However, there are times where using the true horizon line may adversely affect the composition. In the Tuscany Window project on page 116, the horizon line has been slightly lowered to achieve an even balance between land and sky. A higher horizon would have lost most of the sky.

VANISHING POINT The vanishing point is always located on the horizon line. If you were to stand right in the middle of a long straight road, the converging lines formed by the edges of the road would be mirror images of one another, meeting at a point straight ahead of you to make an equilateral triangle.

CONVERGENCE LINES Whenever parallel lines travel away from the viewer, they will appear to converge and move closer together the farther away they are. Eventually they will meet on the horizon at the vanishing point. (If the lines are not parallel and one is traveling toward the other, they will cross each other before the vanishing point.) You will need to work out convergence lines in order to plan architectural features in the foreground, as well as any linear landscape features. To do this, first establish your vanishing point. Fix a piece of string to this point with a piece of masking tape, then stretch the string to the foreground feature; the string marks the convergence line.

PERSPECTIVE IN PRACTICE

⮂ One-point perspective is used in the Stone Archway & Classical Garden mural (page 96) to suggest depth. All the converging lines of the hedges, bushes, lawn, and pond meet at the vanishing point in the temple at the end of the garden. The convergence lines play an important role in the composition also, as the diagonal lines naturally draw the eye in toward the focal point, giving it additional emphasis.

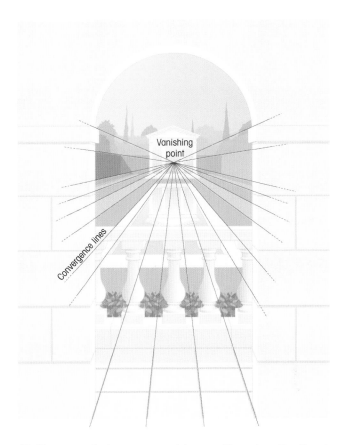

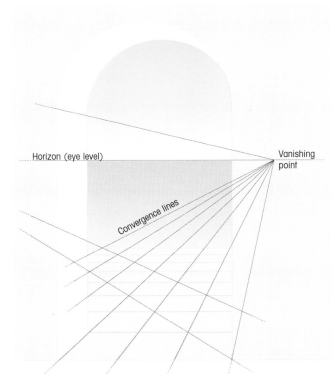

⮂ The vanishing point was established in order to work out the perspective of the balustrades. The bases, equally spaced along the plinth, were planned out first, followed by the tops of each baluster. String was fixed to the vanishing point to plot the back horizontal lines of the blocks. The central baluster is directly beneath the vanishing point, and is thus aligned centrally to the block, but on the other ones, two diagonal lines divide the top surface corner to corner and a vertical line is drawn where they intersect. The other balusters were then aligned to these verticals lines to ensure correct placing.

⮂ If you are placing your mural in a position where it will not usually be viewed head on, it may be more effective to fix your vanishing point at an angle. Here the vanishing point has been moved out of the picture altogether, so that the right inside edge of the archway is obscured, and the left-hand edge appears wider. The grid pattern of the tiling relates to the vanishing point, with the diagonals converging to a point on the right. Remember that the vanishing point will always be on the horizon line.

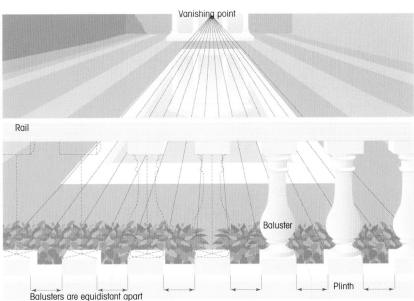

LOUVER DOORS Careful use of perspective is essential for louver windows or doors, but even these require nothing more than the simple, one-point method. Notice that the top and bottom of each slat converges toward the vanishing point, while the horizontal and vertical lines remain constant. The slats above the vanishing point overlap each other slightly, and there is a gap between each slat below the vanishing point. These overlaps and gaps increase the farther they are from the horizon line.

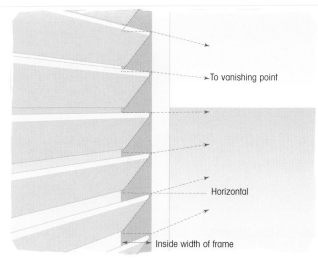

To vanishing point

Horizontal

Inside width of frame

DIMINISHING SIZE

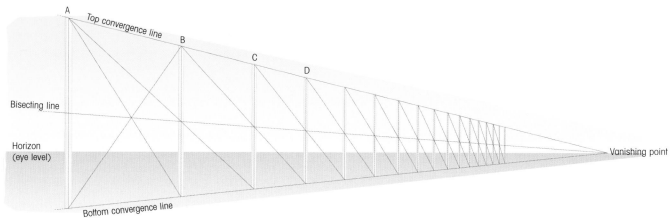

A

Top convergence line

B

C

D

Bisecting line

Horizon
(eye level)

Vanishing point

Bottom convergence line

It is one thing to know that things become smaller as they recede, but sometimes you will need to work out exactly how much smaller, and in what proportion. The diagram above shows you how to make this calculation. The lines could represent fence paneling, terraced houses, or a line of evenly spaced trees, but the method remains the same. The process may initially seem daunting, but it is actually quite simple, and is essential for many trompe l'oeil subjects since an accurate depiction of relative sizes is vital in giving the illusion of space and three dimensions.

First establish your horizon line and the vanishing point, and then draw in the top and bottom convergence lines. Draw two vertical lines (A and B) for the first square or rectangular shape. Then, divide this by drawing two diagonals from corner to corner. Where these diagonals cross, draw a bisecting line all the way to the vanishing point. From the top of line A in the corner, draw another diagonal line to meet the bottom convergence line, passing through the point where the bisecting line crosses line B. Draw another vertical (C) up from the bottom of this diagonal. To draw in vertical D, repeat the process from the top of line B, and continue as many times as necessary.

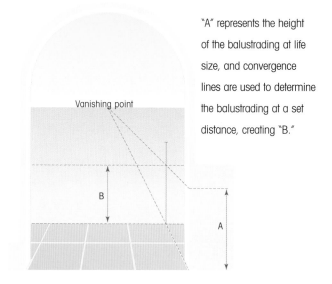

Vanishing point

B

A

"A" represents the height of the balustrading at life size, and convergence lines are used to determine the balustrading at a set distance, creating "B."

TIP When planning a mural your eye will gradually adjust to any slight errors in perspective, preventing you from noticing them. Hold a mirror up to your work so that you see a reflected image. Because this is less familiar, you will be more likely to spot anything that needs altering.

DIVIDING A RECEDING SPACE IN HALF

You may think that this can be done easily by eye, but it is surprising how much smaller the farther half of a space becomes as it recedes. Start with the outer convergence lines, then join the corners with two diagonals, and where these lines cross, draw a horizontal to divide the space in half.

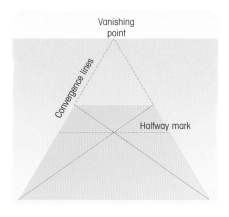

DIVIDING A RECEDING SPACE INTO THIRDS

Begin as shown in the previous diagram, then draw two more diagonal lines from the halfway mark into the opposite corners. At the points where these lines cross the original diagonals, draw two corresponding horizontals lines to divide the area into three. This technique is used to work out the paving in the Stone Archway project on page 96.

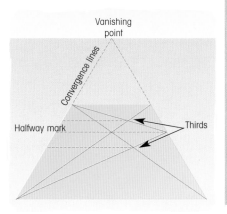

TILING

A tiled floor is made up from a number of equal-sized squares or rectangles, forming a regular grid pattern. Top right you can see that a diagonal line can be drawn passing through the corners of all the squares. The same applies when the floor is seen in perspective (center right). If the convergence lines are drawn in first, the appropriate spacing for the horizontals can be marked where the diagonal crosses the convergence lines.

To achieve diagonal tiling (below right), start with the horizontals as before, then draw in all the diagonals in both directions and erase the horizontals.

To create a convincing effect of the tiles continuing beyond the wall (bottom photograph), it was essential to make the diminishing sizes of the painted tiles on the wall correspond to the real ones on the floor. The first horizontal for the line of tiles was worked out more or less by trial and error, holding a ruler up so that it cut diagonally through the corners of the real tiles to provide the correct angle for the painted ones. The main drawback with such murals is that the trompe l'oeil effect is only convincing from one angle of vision.

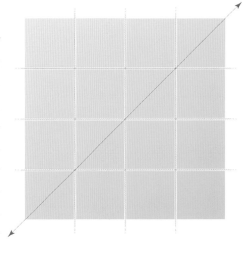

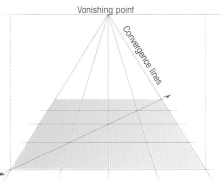

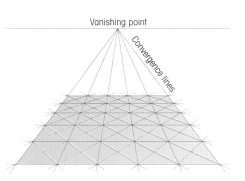

MIXING COLORS

Both the choice of colors and the process of mixing them are very personal matters—artists differ in their approach to color, and all have their own preferred color palettes and individual recipes for useful mixtures. When you begin to try out the projects in this book, you may notice that I tend to use the same colors throughout for mixing, but feel free to experiment with the available range of colors and in time you will discover your own favorites.

MUTED COLORS

A small amount of violet mixed into the main yellow color produces darker yellow tones.

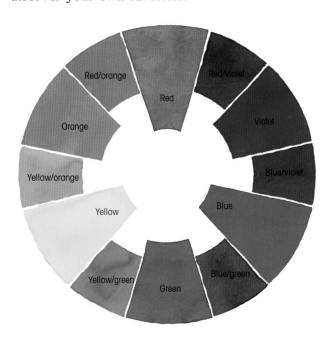

COMPLEMENTARY COLORS

You don't need to make an in-depth study of color theory to choose and mix colors, but it is helpful to have some appreciation of it. As you will see from the color wheel, red and green fall opposite one another, as do yellow and violet, and orange and blue. These opposites are called complementary colors, and they play a very important role in painting, because they have the property of enhancing one another. A yellow flower, for example, will look more vibrant if painted on a violet background, and a red apple will appear more brilliant on a green cloth.

But they have another, seemingly contradictory, use in the context of color mixing, because when mixed they neutralize each other. Mixing equal amounts of red and green produces brown, while mixtures of the other two complementary pairs will yield a range of subtle grays that are much livelier than those mixed from

black and white. You can also mute, or "knock back," a color by adding a little of the complementary—a much more satisfactory method than adding black, which can give a muddy effect.

HARMONIOUS AND CONTRASTING COLORS

The dramatic effects created by contrasting colors are exciting in a small easel painting, but they should be used sparingly in trompe l'oeil murals or they could become overly intrusive. The harmonious colors—those that lie next to each other on the color

HARMONIOUS SEASCAPE

Nature provides us with an abundance of harmonious color schemes, an obvious example being the subtle variations of blue in a seascape. But too much harmony can become bland, so here I have used the bright warm reds of the parrot and the single rose to contrast with the predominantly cool blues.

wheel—may be a better choice, especially for bathroom or bedroom murals where you would probably be aiming for a restful feeling. These colors—orange and yellow, blue and violet, green and blue, and so on—work well together because they share similar bases. You might bring in a touch of complementary contrast if the mural looks too bland, a red flower on the windowsill against a green and blue landscape, for example.

WARM AND COOL COLORS

If you look at the color wheel again you will see that it is divided into two main groups, with the reds, oranges, and yellows on one side and the blues and greens on the other. The reds and yellows, and mixtures of these, are known as warm colors, and they tend to come forward in space, while the blues and greens are perceived as cool, and go back in space.

Of course it is not quite as simple as this because colors do not exist in isolation, and the degree of perceived warmness or coolness is affected to a surprising degree by the surrounding colors. Green, although technically cool, will appear warm when juxtaposed with blue, and blue itself can seem warm against a very cool gray. But once you learn to judge color temperature you will discover how vital it is in creating a sense of space. Because the atmosphere affects the way we see colors, distant hills in a landscape are much cooler in color than foreground features, taking on the hazy blue quality that you can see in many landscape paintings. You can observe this progressive cooling of colors even in the middle distance, with a group of trees set slightly behind another one becoming bluer and less clearly defined.

TIPS

• When mixing pale colors, start with the white and add the darker colors gradually. If you begin with dark colors you may need to add a great deal of white to lighten the mixture.

• Where large amounts of the same color will be needed, always mix more than you think you need; it is very difficult to re-create the exact color.

• Make notes of the quantities and proportions of the colors as you mix them, in case you do need to re-mix.

• Where several similar shades of one color are required, label the mixtures clearly as they may be almost indistinguishable until painted onto the surface.

• Use latex (emulsion) paints as the base color for large areas of your murals as it is more economical.

A SENSE OF SPACE

This mural, with cool blue hills in the distance and warm yellows and browns in the foreground, is a good example of the use of warm and cool colors to create space. The master touch in the depiction of spatial relationships is the bold purple grapes, which makes the eye jump forward to the front of the picture plane.

LIGHT AND SHADOW

Forms are shaped by the way light falls on them. Thus, the quality, strength, and direction of the light are of primary importance in all representational painting. In trompe l'oeil work, a branch of painting in which the illusion relies on a completely realistic depiction of three-dimensional form, light and shadow play an even more vital role.

ESTABLISHING THE LIGHT SOURCE

When you embark on planning a mural, one of the first things to do is to decide where the light source will be, because this will enable you to make the shadows and highlights consistent. Bear this in mind if you are working from several references, all of which may have different light sources. I always try to relate the mural's light source to the one in the room itself in order to create a logical relationship.

Another consideration in this context is the type of mural you are planning. A mural similar to the Stone Urn project (page 90) would have the light source shine "into" the niche from the left or right on the real side of the wall, but in the Tuscany Window project (page 116) the main light source is perceived to be on the other side of the wall, giving the impression of looking out onto a landscape beyond the wall.

CAST SHADOWS

If the light is strong, objects will throw shadows on the surface beneath them, or on other objects nearby. These will vary according to the position of the light source—at midday on a sunny day, the shadows are very short or even non-existent because the sun is overhead, but a low early-morning or late-afternoon light produces long, slanting shadows. This play of light picks out and highlights forms, often transforming a landscape from a flat expanse into a scene that is full of color and previously unsuspected detail. When you come to plan your mural you will need to consider whether you want this kind of dramatic effect or a more subtle one produced by hazy sunlight or a high sun.

CHANGING SHADOWS

Compare the shadows cast by the balustrading in these two murals. The mural above shows a noonday or mid-afternoon light. The sun is high enough in the sky that the balustrade only casts a small strip of shadow. The beach scene below appears to be much later in the afternoon. As the sun sinks lower in the sky, the shadows cast by the balustrade are almost long enough to mirror its shape.

SURFACE LIGHT

There are two types of light and shadow that can be used to suggest the solidity of an object. One is the light that falls on the surface of the object, which is dictated by the position of the object in relation to the light source. The light-struck areas of a form will be higher in tone—paler—than those that turn away from the light, so it is important to pay as much attention to tone as you do to color. The tonal gradations vary according to the form. For example, they will be quite gentle on a rounded form, merging into one another with no hard boundaries, but on a straight-sided form such as a box the gradations will be very much sharper and more distinct.

It is not always easy to assess tone because the eye registers colors without initially taking in how light or dark they are, so you will need to observe carefully in order to suggest light and shadow convincingly. Study real objects whenever you can, and if you find it hard to identify the different tones, try half-closing your eyes, which cuts out much of the detail and reduces the impact of the color. Look also at objects with different textures, as texture has an important influence on how light affects tone. For example, a polished china vase will have sharp highlights and very dark shadows, but on a matte-surfaced object such as a terra-cotta urn or a piece of rough fabric the highlights will be soft and diffused and the shadows less distinct.

TONAL VALUES

This photograph shows how light affects the tonal values on three different-shaped objects. The cast shadows slant to the right because light is coming from the upper left. Another factor that needs to be taken into account is indirect reflected light, which bounces off the surfaces of one object onto another. The different tones of an object can be broken down into shadows, mid tones, and highlights, terms that are used throughout the project sections of the book in relation to color mixing.

SHADOW COLOR

Although tone is the first consideration when modeling form, color also plays a vital role. Avoid using black or gray for shadows, as these two colors will make the mural look flat and dull. A useful strategy is gradually to mix in some of the contrasting color to that of the object. For example, if you were mixing a shadow color for a light purple object or surface, you could simply add more purple, but, although this would deepen the tone, it would also make the color bolder. Adding some yellow, which is the contrasting—or complementary—color, in conjunction with the purple will have the effect of muting the purple so that it is pushed back in space.

Shadows on white surfaces have a very subtle blue-gray tone. One of my own recipes for these shadows is a mixture of flesh tint, cobalt blue, and white, but you will discover your own in time, so experiment with various mixtures and note any interesting color combinations.

ELEMENTS

ELEMENTS

THE ELEMENTS IN THIS CHAPTER HAVE BEEN CHOSEN MAINLY FOR THEIR VERSATILITY. MOST OF THEM CAN BE USED ON THEIR OWN, OR AS PART OF A LARGER TROMPE L'OEIL MURAL. ONCE YOU ARE FAMILIAR WITH THE TECHNIQUES, THEY ARE FAIRLY SIMPLE TO ACHIEVE, AND YOU CAN THEN VARY THEM AS YOU WISH TO CREATE NEW EFFECTS.

STONE
BLOCKING

STONE BLOCKING IS SIMPLE BUT VERSATILE. IT CAN BE USED ON ITS OWN AS AN OVER-ALL PAINT EFFECT, IDEAL FOR ADDING INTEREST AND FORMALITY TO A COURTYARD OR HALLWAY, AND WORKS WELL AS PART OF A MURAL TO ENHANCE OTHER TROMPE L'OEIL ARCHITECTURAL FEATURES, SUCH AS COLUMNS AND BALUSTRADES (SEE STONE ARCHWAY & CLASSICAL GARDEN PROJECT, PAGES 96–105). BEFORE ATTEMPTING A WHOLE WALL, EXPERIMENT ON A SMALL AREA OR A PANEL TO FAMILIARIZE YOURSELF WITH THE TECHNIQUES.

BLOCK LENGTH ADJUSTMENT

$$\frac{Length\ of\ room}{Length\ of\ block} = X$$

X rounded to the nearest half or whole = Y

$$\frac{Length\ of\ room}{Y} = New\ block\ length$$

New adjusted block length

Length of wall	109 in (277cm)
Block length	17 in (43cm)

109 in ÷ 17 in = 6.4, round to 6.5
(277cm ÷ 43cm = 6.4, round to 6.5)

109 in ÷ 6.5 = 16.77 = 16¾ in
(277cm ÷ 6.5 = 42.5cm)

New adjusted block height

Height of wall	80 in (203cm)
Block height	12 in (30cm)

80 in ÷ 12 in = 6.7, round to 7
(203cm ÷ 30cm = 6.7, round to 7)

80 in ÷ 7 = 11.4 = 11½ in
(203cm ÷ 7 = 29cm)

The dimensions of the adjusted block are 16¾ x 11½ in (42.5 x 29cm)

PREPARATION

The first step is to measure the area to be painted. A stone block is roughly 17 x 12 inches (43 x 30cm). It is unlikely these dimensions will divide neatly into the desired area, so slight adjustments may be required. First measure the length of the area, then divide this number by the proposed length of the block, here 17 inches (43cm). (Always remember to use like measurements— either inches or centimeters). Round this number to the nearest whole or half number. Divide the length of the area by the rounded number, and the result is the new adjusted block length.

The height of the block can be worked out in the same way, however the numbers are rounded to whole numbers only. (Rows of blocks will be staggered; half a block at the end of a row will look normal, but half a row at the bottom or top will not.) Be prepared for a degree of compromise around doors and windows.

COLOR PALETTE

When mixing colors, always ensure that you have enough to finish the mural—it is better to over- rather than under-estimate, as it is almost impossible to mix exactly the same shade again.

For the first wash color, start by mixing together some Raw Sienna and Yellow Ochre with a larger quantity of Pure White in the bottom of a large paint pot or plastic cup. At this stage you only need to fill about 5–10 percent of the pot. Add a small quantity of Raw Umber to tone down the yellow, and mix the paint with a spare brush. When you are satisfied with the shade—bearing in mind that it will be lighter on the wall—gradually add

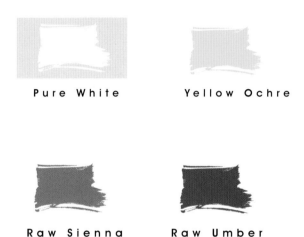

Pure White   **Yellow Ochre**

Raw Sienna   **Raw Umber**

water in a ratio of about 15 parts water to 1 part paint, mixing continuously to ensure that all the paint is equally diluted. You may need to make adjustments, so add the water gradually, testing the color out on a spare part of the wall as you go along.

The mid-tone color can be mixed in a smaller pot, using the same colors as before but with less Pure White and more Raw Umber. Again mix in some water, but this time in a 1:1 ratio. Note: If you intend to paint trompe l'oeil effects over the stone blocking, for example foliage, keep some of the mid-tone color, as you will need it for shadows.

For the deep tone, use Raw Umber alone, mixing it with a small amount of water in a small pot. Mix Pure White with a little Yellow Ochre and Raw Sienna in another small pot for the highlight tone, again adding a small quantity of water.

In this example a base coat of white latex (emulsion) paint has been laid over the whole of the wall. Different results can be obtained by laying a color other than white. A darker base coat will result in a commensurately darker shade of stonework.

STEP
BY STEP

STEP 1 ▲▲▲

Using a level, draw a faint vertical line in charcoal or light pencil and mark off the heights of the blocks, then draw in horizontal lines corresponding to the marks along the length of the wall. Next, mark off the widths of the blocks along one horizontal line, and use the level to draw vertical lines up to the next horizontal line. This will be the first row of blocks.

The stone blocks are staggered, so the next stage is to measure halfway along each one and draw in the vertical lines for the next row. It is now a straightforward task to draw in all the remaining rows of blocks by positioning the level against a vertical line, skipping a row, and drawing in the vertical lines on the next row.

STEP 2

With a ¼-inch (6mm) flat brush and the mid-tone color, paint in a thick grout line over the charcoal line using the level as a guide. Adjust the pressure on the brush occasionally to give the line some variation. When using the level as a guide for painting straight lines, keep the bristles away from the wall edge of the level, otherwise the paint may bleed down the back. You also need to keep the level itself clean and paint-free to avoid smudging on paint when you position it on the next part of the wall.

STEP 3 ▲ ▲ ▲

Vary the grout line by curving some of the intersections between the horizontal and vertical lines, achieving slightly rounded corners. Differ the curves a little to give each block an individual look. Leave to dry.

TIP

Dungarees or an old shirt with a breast pocket large enough to hold a small plastic cup of paint are handy attire when it comes to painting with a level. With the paint in your pocket, your hands are free to hold the brush and the level, and you can reload the brush without moving away from the wall. However, make sure that the paint cup is less than a quarter full, and remember to remove it before bending over!

STEP 4 ▲ ▲ ▲

Using the color wash and a large decorator's brush, softly brush in the color, working it in all directions. Don't overload the brush or you will be constantly chasing drips and runs, and try not to leave any obvious brushmarks. If you find this difficult, use a stippling brush or a sponge instead. Alternatively, you could use a slightly less watery paint mix to wash over the blocks individually, stopping at the grout lines.

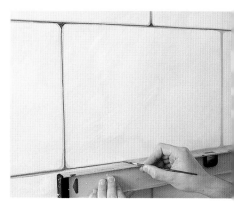

STEP 5 ▲ ▲ ▲

In the middle of the large grout line (where the original charcoal line was) add the final grout line using a No. 1 round brush and the Raw Umber paint mix. As before, use the level as a guide to paint the straight lines. Work freehand to curve the corners, leaving a squashed triangle shape in the grout.

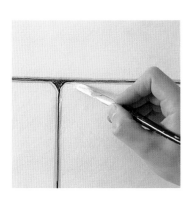

STEP 6 ▲ ▲ ▲

Decide on your light source, which will usually be either upper left or upper right. Use a medium brush to add the highlights on each block, painting up to the edge of the mid-tone grout line. Here the light source is coming from the upper left, so the top and left edges of each block are highlighted.

FINISH ▲ ▲ ▲

The age and condition of your sandstone can be varied to suit location and atmosphere. A small "blemish" has been added to the face of the lower left block with some highlighting and shading.

VARIATION ▼ ▼ ▼

A simple marble effect. The base color is a mixture of Pure White with a little Burnt Sienna and Raw Umber. The veining is a mix of Pure White and diluted Raw Umber, and is applied with a flat brush.

STEP 7 ▲ ▲ ▲

To add a chip, use a flat brush and the mid-tone color to lightly dab or flick in a brushstroke. Smudge the paint down toward the edge of the block with your finger. Thicken the darker grout line at this point and add a highlight at the bottom.

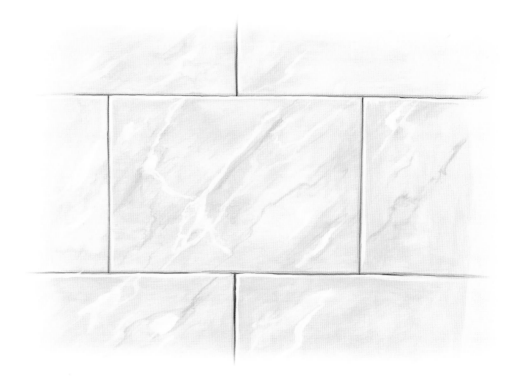

DRAPE

TROMPE L'OEIL DRAPERY SOFTENS ARCHITECTURAL FEATURES, BOTH PAINTED AND REAL, AND TROMPE L'OEIL WINDOWS. OFTEN USED TO HIDE OR CONCEAL THINGS, DRAPES ALSO CREATE A THEATRICAL, DRAMATIC ATMOSPHERE. ONCE YOU HAVE LEARNED TO PAINT CONVINCING DRAPERY FOLDS, YOU CAN EMPLOY THE SAME TECHNIQUES TO PAINT CLOTHING OR ANY OTHER DECORATIVE OR DOMESTIC FABRICS, FROM A BEACH TOWEL DRYING ON A BALCONY, TO A SILK SCARF THROWN OVER THE BACK OF A CHAIR.

COLOR PALETTE

The drape in this example has been painted in a bold yellow, but you can choose any color you please. The paint used is latex (emulsion) paint, which is a practical and economical choice for any mural that uses a lot of the same color—a skyscape, for example. Bulk mixing emulsion saves a lot of time, as it means you will have enough of the color to finish the mural without having to remix.

First mix the Yellow latex (emulsion) with water in a pot at a ratio of about 2:1. For the mid tone, add a small amount of Dioxazine Purple to the yellow, plus a little extra water. Mix in more Dioxazine Purple for the darkest tone, and for the highlight color, mix Yellow with Pure White.

Yellow

Dioxazine
Purple

Pure White

STEP
BY STEP

STEP 1 ▲ ▲ ▲

Using a light charcoal pencil, begin by sketching a very faint outline of the drape, curving the line down and around, and drawing a tie-back about two-thirds of the way down. Beneath this, drop the line down more vertically and make a series of zigzagging curves for the bottom edge of the drape, going from the right side toward the back. Draw a small, almost vertical line upward from each curve to suggest the folds in the fabric.

Using a round or flat brush well-loaded with the darkest color, paint in the line. Then add some loose fold lines starting wide apart at the top and converging into a bunch toward the tie-back. Paint in some fold lines at the bottom of the drape, varying the lines by adjusting the brush pressure to avoid a uniform, striped look. Leave to dry.

STEP 2 ▲ ▲ ▲

Block in the whole of the drape with the yellow base color using a small decorator's brush. The linear underpainting should remain visible beneath the new color.

STEP 3 ▶ ▶ ▶

Gradually build up the depth of color and the shadows, using the mid tone and the base yellow. Pay attention to the light source, which dictates where the shadows will be cast, especially on the zigzag folds at the bottom of the drape. In this example, the light is coming from the top right.

STEP 5 ▼ ▼ ▼

Finally, use the darkest tone again to add some shadows to give the impression of tighter folds in the fabric. These darker shadows are mainly in the area around the tie-back, where the fabric is bunched up. Add some highlights to the light-catching parts of the folds, again paying attention to the light source. In this example, the area around the drape has been darkened, both to suggest cast shadows and to make the highlights stand out more strongly.

STEP 4 ▲ ▲ ▲

Continue to accentuate the folds using both the mid tone and the darkest color. Let the brushstrokes follow the direction of the folds.

FINISH ◀◀◀

This elegant drape is classic in style, and understated. Tassled ends, a more ostentatious tie-back, or simply a change in color—perhaps a rich red or royal blue—can quickly give your drape a more dramatic look.

▲▲▲
VARIATION 1

The sea breeze has caught the long drape that helps to soften the square features of the opening and louver doors.

▼▼▼
VARIATION 2

Enveloped in drapery and flanked with angels, God casually reaches out to have his wine glass refilled, in this play on Michelangelo's *The Creation of Adam*.

BALUSTRADING

BALUSTRADING LENDS ELEGANCE, BALANCE, AND RHYTHM TO A MURAL. IT ACTS AS AN ATTRACTIVE BOUNDARY WITHOUT ACTUALLY INTERFERING TOO MUCH WITH THE FLOW OF THE MURAL'S BACKGROUND, WHICH CAN BE VIEWED IN BETWEEN THE BALUSTERS. IT ALSO PROVIDES A HANDY PLACE TO SITE A TROMPE L'OEIL GLASS OF WINE, OR PERHAPS A COLORFUL PARROT.

COLOR PALETTE

Mix a little Cobalt Blue into the Flesh Tint to make a dark pinkish gray, then mix varying amounts of Pure White to this color so that you have a range of four tones, from a dark to a highlight color. The latter should be mainly white, with just a little of the basic pinkish gray. Add a small quantity of water to each mix to help the paint flow.

Cobalt Blue

Flesh Tint

Pure White

This balustrade outline can be scaled up and used as a template.

STEP
BY STEP

STEP 1 ▶ ▶ ▶

Design your own template, or scale up the image on the page opposite (see pages 32–33). Transfer the design to your wall (see pages 34–35). Using the mid-tone color and a small round brush, paint over all the outlines.

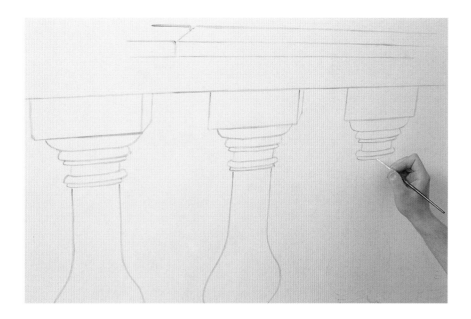

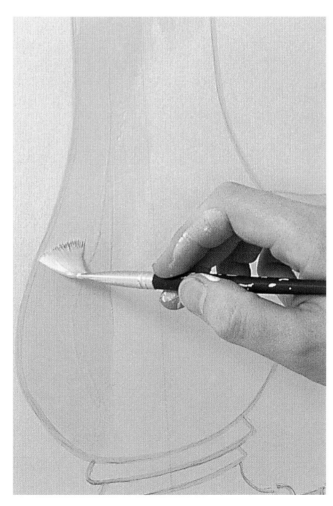

STEP 2 ▲ ▲ ▲

Use the light tone and a ⅝-inch (16mm) flat brush to block in the balustrade, making sure that the painted outline is still visible.

STEP 3 ▲ ▲ ▲

Using both the light tone and the mid tone, start forming the shadow on the baluster. Decide on the light source—here the light comes from top left—and paint the mid tone down the right-hand side. Keep to the shape of the edges, and then curve the line of shadow down and under, thickening it as you go. Gradually bring the color toward the middle of the baluster, blending it into the light tone. Add a thinner shadow on the left-hand edge to emphasize the curvature, blending it in as before.

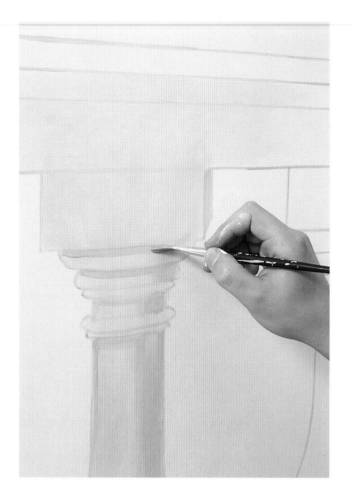

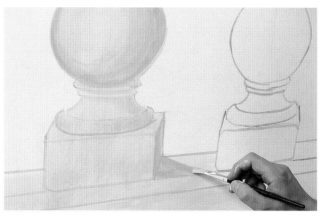

STEP 4 ◀◀◀   ▲▲▲

Add shadows under the moldings, beneath the rail of the balustrading, and at the bottom of each baluster. Thinking about the direction of the light, paint the shadows cast by each column on the lower balustrading; in this case the shadows form a triangle shape on the right-hand side.

STEP 5 ▶▶▶

Use the dark tone with the mid tone to pick out the finer detailing with a fine round brush. Add sharper shadows under the moldings, and then repeat step 3, making a thin line of the dark tone around the edge and blending it into the mid tone.

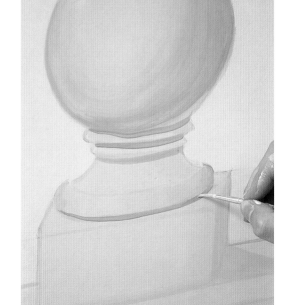

STEP 6 ▲▲▲

Using the very pale color and the flat brush, paint in the highlights off-center toward the edge near the light, and blend them in.

STEP 7 ▶ ▶ ▶

Add highlights to the top of the rail, the top of the base block, and the top edges of the moldings. If you wish, you can add tints to the finished work to give the stonework more color variation, using diluted mixes of the Flesh Tint and/or Cobalt Blue. Experiment with other colors to see what different effects can be achieved; for example you could try adding a wash with Pure White and Raw Umber. You might also wish to add some stone chips and cracks here and there to give the balustrade a more aged appearance.

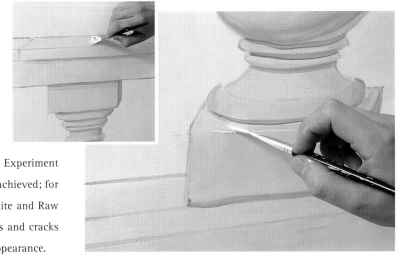

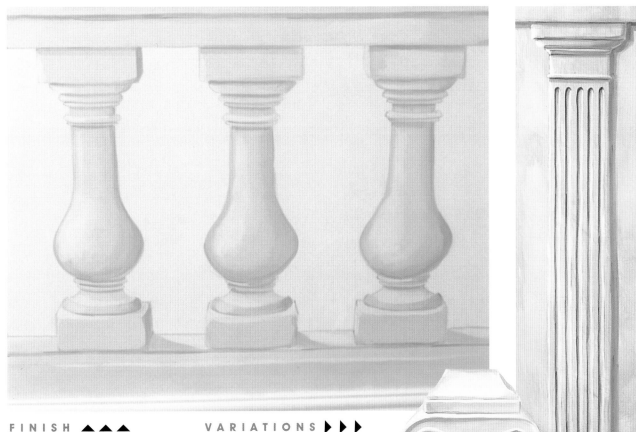

FINISH ▲ ▲ ▲

Notice that in a row of balusters, each one will be slightly different. The sides of the center baluster are not visible, while the left and right baulsters show their right and left sides restpectively. Note also the converging join line in the rail.

VARIATIONS ▶ ▶ ▶

A baluster is really an oddly shaped pillar or plinth. Pilasters with flat surfaces (right) are quite straightforward as long as you pay attention to the highlights and cast shadows. The fluting effect is measured, then painted with the shadow and highlight tones using a level as a guide.

CRUMBLING
WALL

MARBLING AND OTHER PAINT EFFECTS SUGGEST LUXURY AND EXTRAVAGANCE, BUT OLD BRICKWORK HAS SPECIAL CHARMS OF ITS OWN. ALONE, IT CREATES AN INFORMAL, RELAXED ATMOSPHERE—IDEAL FOR A CONSERVATORY OR SUN-BAKED WALL—AND AS PART OF A LARGER MURAL SETS A RUSTIC SCENE. PAINTED AROUND AN EXISTING FEATURE, SUCH AS A WALL LIGHT, IT CAN BE VERY EFFECTIVE; THE SUGGESTION THAT THE PLASTER HAS BEEN WEAKENED AROUND THIS POINT LENDING CREDULITY TO THE *TROMPE*.

COLOR PALETTE

To create the wall-effect wash, first mix an equal quantity of Raw Umber and Raw Sienna with a larger quantity of Pure White in a large plastic cup, gradually adding about 15 parts of water. For the shadow color, use an equal amount of Raw Umber, Raw Sienna and Pure White mixed with an equal quantity of water. For the brick color, use Burnt Sienna mixed with a smaller amount of Raw Umber, mixing in 5–6 parts water, again gradually. Make a darker brick color by mixing Raw Umber and Cobalt Blue diluted with about 8 parts water. For the mortar color, use Pure White and a little Raw Umber mixed with an equal amount of water, and for the highlight color, mix a little Raw Sienna into Pure White with a small amount of water.

Raw Sienna

Cobalt Blue

Raw Umber

Burnt Sienna

Pure White

STEP
BY STEP

STEP 1 ▶▶▶

With a large decorator's brush, pick up a small amount of the wash color and gradually brush it in all directions. Make sure you catch any drips, and avoid leaving any obvious brushmarks. Leave this first coat to dry before washing on a second layer. An interesting effect can be created at this stage by altering the pressure on the brush. Increasing the pressure will remove the first layer of paint, creating a patchy effect that can be softened by washing over again with a very light pressure.

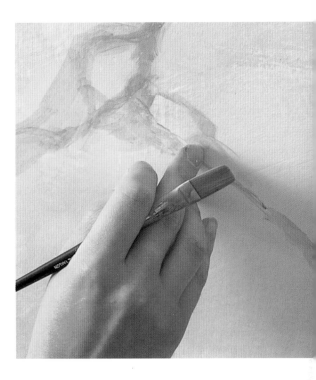

STEP 2 ▼▼▼

Using a ⅝-inch (16mm) flat brush well loaded with the shadow color, sketch in the rough outline of the crumbled area. Try to keep this near to the top left- or right-hand side of the wall, and make the edges deliberately uneven by adjusting the pressure on the brush and twisting it slightly here and there to thin out or thicken the line.

STEP 3 ▲▲▲

Bring the edges of this shape loosely together and paint a thick crack diagonally down toward the center of the wall, using a "tickling" technique with the brush, twisting it here and there to adjust the line thickness. Use your finger to smudge the paint in places, especially if the line is becoming too defined, and make some circular—but not too circular—motions with the brush to create a little cluster of crumbled wall where a crack might split off into two directions. The flat brush will give this a more angular look. You can add some crumbling around the edge of the brick area also, but don't overdo it. Again use your finger to smudge the paint wherever necessary.

STEP 4 ▶ ▶ ▶

Load a smaller decorator's brush with the brick color and gradually build up the color in the area within the painted crumble line, allowing the paint to dry between each coat. Use the darker brick color in small amounts to dull down the terra-cotta color here and there. It can also be used to rub off some of the color, as suggested in step 1, which will create a more faded look.

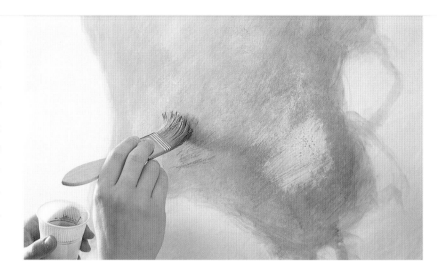

STEP 5 ◀ ◀ ◀

Use a level and a brick template, which can be made from stiff cardboard, to draw the brick shapes onto the wall with a charcoal pencil. A good template size is 8 x 2½ inches (20 x 6cm). Leave a gap between the bricks of approximately ½ inch (1.5cm). Stagger the rows, but don't be too concerned about accuracy. Cut the corners off some of the bricks to heighten the effect, and vary the sizes a little as well.

STEP 6 ▶ ▶ ▶

Pick up some of the mortar color on a ½-inch (13mm) flat brush and loosely paint in the mortar, leaving the paint patchy in places and occasionally using your finger to smudge it. Overly neat lines will ruin the effect.

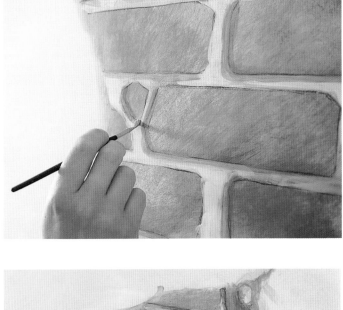

STEP 7 ▶ ▶ ▶

The next step is to add shading. In this example the light source is coming from the upper right side, so the shadows are painted adjacent to the bottom and left-hand edges of each brick. Using the shadow color, paint the shadow cast on the mortar by the individual bricks with a No. 3 round brush. Varying the thickness suggests that some bricks jut farther out from the mortar than others. Once again, use your finger to smudge some of the shadows.

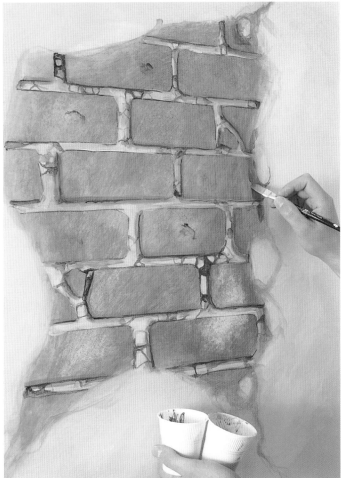

STEP 8 ▲ ▲ ▲

Using a No. 1 or 3 round brush and some Raw Umber mixed with a little water, add some chips and cracks to the mortar. You can block in some slightly larger areas with Raw Umber to suggest that the mortar has fallen out in places. As in step 3, tickle with the brush and smudge with your finger.

STEP 9 ▲ ▲ ▲

Now the bricks appear to sit back into the wall slightly. Use the Raw Umber and the brick color with the ⅝-inch (16mm) flat brush to add a shadow to the top and right edge of the bricked area. With the shadow color, darken the edges where the plaster meets the brickwork to further build up the illusion of depth.

STEP 10 ▶ ▶ ▶

Pick up some Raw Umber on a small fine crack within the loose cracks achieved in steps 2 and 3. This will have the effect of deepening them. Experiment with both brushes to see which effect you prefer. Also work around the edges of the brick area, darkening the shadows in places to enhance the illusion of the bricks being set back into the wall. Smudge the line in places with your finger or a rag.

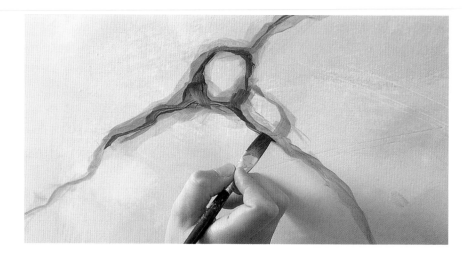

Step 11 ▼ ▼ ▼

You can add chips in the wall using both the shadow and highlight colors. In this example a large chip has been painted around the cracks, using the shadow color for the top right edge and the highlight color for the bottom left edge, corresponding with the light source at upper right. For smaller chips, paint the first half of the shape in the shadow tone and smudge it toward the inside of the shape to leave the outside edge more defined, and then add the highlight color. Finally, add the highlight color to the bottom and left of the exposed brick area along the edge of the crumbling plasterwork and along the bottom edges of the cracks. If you wish, add some more of the wash color used in step 1, perhaps mixing up a slightly different tone.

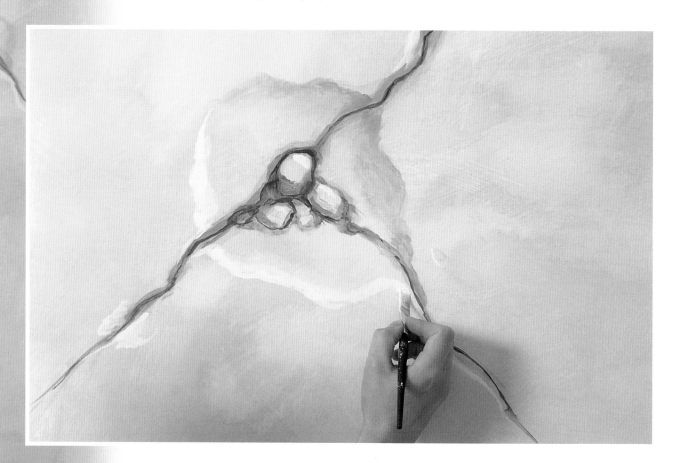

FINISH ▶ ▶ ▶

This informal effect is one you can make your own, and it will probably look a little different every time you paint it.

▲ ▲ ▲

VARIATION 1

An aged mural has crumbled and broken away in places to reveal the stone wall beneath.

◀ ◀ ◀

VARIATION 2

Foliage creeps through and over this decayed brick wall, and the boundary between inside and oustside is blurred.

GREENERY

This ivy outline can be used as a template, but if possible, find some real ivy to refer to as you paint.

GREENERY CAN TAKE MANY FORMS, FROM A SINGLE LEAF TO LUXURIOUS FOLIAGE OR A GROUP OF DISTANT TREES. THE TERM "GREENERY" ITSELF IS MISLEADING, AS GREEN IS ONLY ONE OF THE MANY COLORS PRESENT IN FOLIAGE, AND EVEN THEY VARY GREATLY. THE SEASONS BRING IN FURTHER VARIATIONS, WITH THE BRILLIANT YELLOW-GREENS OF SPRING AND THE RICH ORANGES AND REDS OF FALL.

Two types of greenery are offered here—the individual, distinct leaves of a creeping ivy vine, and clumps of foliage, found on a bush or hedge.

COLOR PALETTE

Start by mixing the two background colors. In one pot, mix Chromium Oxide Green with a little water, and in another pot, mix the same color with a little Mars Black. Next, make two lighter colors, again using the Chromium Oxide Green, but mixing it with Leaf Green, Cadmium Yellow and Pure White. Again, avoid adding too much water—you only need just enough to help the paint flow better from the brush. You will also need the shadow color that was used to paint the balustrade (see page 56).

Chromium Oxide Green

Leaf Green

Mars Black

Pure White

Cadmium Yellow

FOLIAGE

FOLIAGE PAINTED BEHIND A BALUSTRADE—DEEP GREENS AGAINST STONEWORK—ADDS AN ELEMENT OF CONTRAST THAT DEFINES THE ARCHITECTURAL DETAILING. THE DEEP GREENS WILL ALSO SUGGEST DEPTH BEYOND THE BALUSTRADING, ENHANCING THE TROMPE L'OEIL EFFECT.

STEP
BY STEP

STEP 1 ▼▼▼

Because the greenery is painted behind the balustrade, special care must be taken with the edges. Using the lighter background color and a flat artist's brush, cut in around the edges first, and then brush the paint in all directions.

◀◀◀

STEP 2

With a small decorator's brush, stipple in a little of the darker background color. Leave to dry.

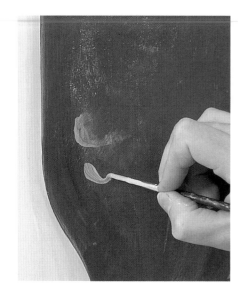

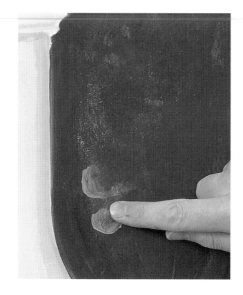

STEP 3 ▲▲▲

Start painting the leaves with one of the lighter green mixes, using a small round brush to paint the front of the leaf shape.

STEP 4 ▲▲▲

Smudge the paint upward with your finger, leaving a defined edge at the bottom. This gives the impression that the front of the leaf is catching the light while the rest is in shadow. Continue to build up the leaves in the same way, varying the greens.

STEP 5 ▲▲▲

Carry some leaves over the balustrading, using different-sized flat brushes. These are ideal for foliage, as they enable you to create varied leaf shapes with just one or two short brushstrokes. Finally, add some cast shadows on the balustrade, using the shadow color and the same flat brushes.

FINISH ◀◀◀

The foliage adds depth and definition to the balustrades. The addition of a few random flowers could add extra color if desired.

IVY

THE STONE BLOCKING PAINTED EARLIER (SEE PAGES 46–49) IS USED AS THE BACKGROUND FOR THIS SIMPLE EFFECT, BUT YOU COULD EASILY PAINT IT ON A PLAIN WALL. IF YOU DECIDE TO USE THE STONE WALL, DON'T OVERSTATE THE IVY—PERHAPS RESTRICT IT TO JUST A FEW STRANDS CREEPING IN FROM THE CORNERS. TRY TO FIND SOME REAL IVY TO REFER TO WHILE PAINTING, OR MAKE PRELIMINARY STUDIES AND USE EITHER SKETCHES OR PHOTOGRAPHS.

COLOR PALETTE

Mix Chromium Oxide Green with a little water in one pot. In another, mix Chromium Oxide Green, Leaf Green, and a little Pure White. Mix a lighter green for the leaf veins, using Pure White mixed with a little Chromium Oxide Green. If you are painting the ivy on the stone blocking, you will also need some of the mid-tone color used previously (see p 47).

Pure White

Leaf Green

Chromium Oxide Green

STEP
BY STEP

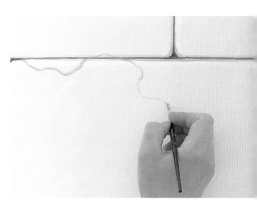

STEP 1 ▶▶▶
If you have obtained some ivy leaves, use masking tape to stick them onto a nearby area of the wall for reference. Using a small round brush and the two darker greens, begin by painting a wavy stem weaving in and out of the grout line. Try to give the lines a flowing, natural feel.

STEP 2 ▲▲▲
Now paint some lines curving away from the stem. Repeat these along the whole length, but make the lines shorter toward the end of the stem. Sketch or trace an ivy leaf shape around these lines, keeping the line as the center stem of the leaf.

STEP 3 ◀◀◀

Block in the leaves using the darker green. Allow to dry before deciding whether it is necessary to lay on a further coat of green.

STEP 4 ▶▶▶

Using the lightest green and a very fine round brush, add the veining to each leaf. Start by painting over the original curved center line, and then radiate the lines outward to the edges of the leaf. It is important to get the veining right, so study your reference as you work.

STEP 5 ◀◀◀

Use some of the mid-tone color mixed for the stone blocking to add some cast shadows on the wall. Curve them slightly away from the leaves to give the impression that the tips of the leaves point away from the wall surface.

FINISH ▲▲▲

Meandering ivy lends a contrast to the uniformity of stone blocking. (See Sky Ceiling with Foliage, pages 76–81, to see this effect taken a stage further.)

VARIATION 1 ▼▼▼

Foliage climbs through ancient rubble in the foreground, and trees have grown around a temple in the distance.

VARIATION 2 ▲▲▲

Flowers are another element of foliage. Roses like these are painted with just a few flat-brush crescent strokes and highlighting.

LOUVER
DOORS

ADDING A PAIR OF OPEN LOUVER DOORS TO A TROMPE L'OEIL WINDOW CAN ENHANCE THE FEELING OF DEPTH. THE CONVERGING PERSPECTIVE LINES LEAD THE EYE TO WHAT LIES OUTSIDE, WHETHER IT BE A MEDITERRANEAN LANDSCAPE, A GROUP OF TREES IN THE MIDDLE DISTANCE, OR A POT OF FLOWERS ON A BALCONY. THE GAPS IN THE INDIVIDUAL SLATS ALSO OFFER A TANTALIZING GLIMPSE OF WHAT LIES BEYOND. THIS ELEMENT, IN WHICH PERSPECTIVE IS ALL-IMPORTANT, REQUIRES CAREFUL PLANNING, SO TRY TO FIND SOME VISUAL REFERENCE IF POSSIBLE.

COLOR PALETTE

Latex (emulsion) paint is used in this example, with Medium Green as the base color. Mix some Pure White into the green in one pot to lighten it, and in another pot, make the highlight color by adding more white. For the shadow tone, put some of the base green into another pot, and mix in some Red Oxide and Chromium Oxide Green.

Medium Green

Pure White

Red Oxide

Chromium Oxide Green

STEP
BY STEP

Converging lines

Leave a gap (roughly ¼ in (6mm) between the door spine and edge of window

Vanishing point

Horizon

Center vertical

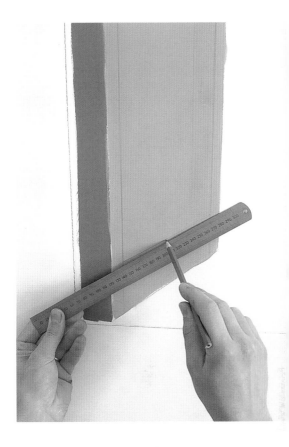

STEP 1 ▲▲▲

Begin by planning the window. If there are other windows in the room it is a good idea to use their measurements as a guide. Establish the horizon and center vertical lines, and mark the vanishing point (see Perspective, page 36). Draw two long vertical rectangles, one on the inside right and one on the inside left of the window, 1–1½ inches wide (25-38mm) and leaving a gap of about ¼ inch (6mm) between this rectangle and the edge of window. These are the spines of the doors. Fix a piece of string at the vanishing point and draw in the top and bottom edges of the door. Because of the foreshortening, the door will appear to be narrower. In this example the doors are opened at a right angle to the window. As a general rule of thumb, the width of the door will appear to be about one-fifth of the distance from the window's edge to the center vertical.

STEP 2 ▶▶▶

In this example, the light is coming from the right, striking the door face. Block in the door using the shadow tone on the spine and the light green on the door face.

STEP 3 ▶▶▶

When the paint is dry, draw in the door frame with a pencil, using the level for the verticals and the string for the diagonals at the top and bottom. Remember that because of the perspective effect, the top and bottom frames will appear to be thicker than the sides, and the nearer one (on the left side of the door in this example) thicker than the one at the back. Make the bottom frame slightly thicker than the top one to give a sense of balance.

STEP 4 ▶▶▶

Now draw a faint vertical line showing the inside of the far frame, with the pencil held against the level. Make the thickness of this part of the frame slightly narrower than the thickness of the spine.

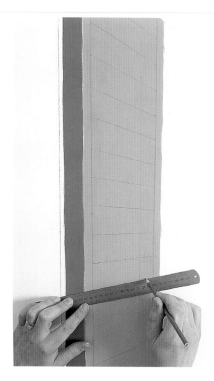

STEP 6 ▲▲▲

Now hold the piece of string firmly across these points, mark off the corresponding ones on the near side of the door, and join the marks with a pencil and ruler.

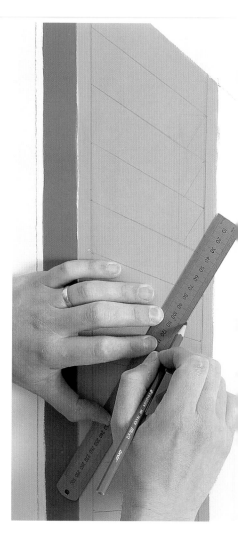

STEP 5 ▲▲▲

Measure the height of the inside of the frame at the furthest end (in this case the right-hand side), and divide this by 1½ inches (4cm), rounding the figure up or down to a whole one. This gives you the number of louvers on the door. Divide the height of the inside of the frame again by this new figure to give the louver spacing. Transfer this measurement onto a piece of paper or card. For example, if the measurement is 1¼ inches (3cm), make a series of marks this distance apart, then hold this up to the vertical of the frame and mark them off one by one. If the paper is not long enough for the whole of the height just reapply it farther down. If measured correctly, the inside of the frame will now be divided up into equal heights.

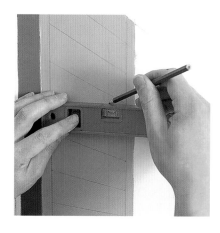

STEP 7 ▲▲▲

The next stage is to start plotting the slanted edges of the louvers. Using a level held horizontally against the markings made in step 5, make faint corresponding marks down the vertical line drawn in step 4. (See diagram on page 38.)

STEP 8 ▲▲▲

Use a ruler and pencil to join the marks, making a series of diagonals running downward from the vertical of the back door frame. Do not fully join up the lines at the top half of the door, as they will overlap the converging louver lines— finish the line where it meets the other line. Where the lines meet the vertical one achieved in step 4, draw the other side of the louvers, again using the string. You will notice that the louvers appear to overlap at the top of the door, while seeming farther apart toward the bottom. If the doors were overlooking a landscape, parts of it would be visible through these gaps.

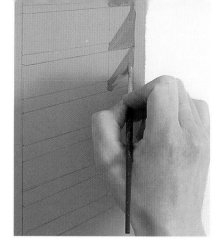

STEP 9 ▲▲▲

Using a small round brush and the shadow tone, paint in the saw-edge pattern at the ends of the louvers, then add in some more fine shadows underneath the top frame and at the top and bottom of the far frame. Paint in the individual slats with the green base color using a ⅝-inch (16mm) flat brush.

STEP 10 ▼▼▼

With a No. 3 round brush and the lightest color, highlight the top edge of each louver, resting the brush against a straight edge. Paint the background between the slats on the bottom half of the door. Add hinges on the spines. The gap between the top hinge and the top of the door should be greater than that between the bottom hinge and the bottom of the door. The part of the hinge attached to the window is foreshortened, so check the angle, then draw the swivel part of the hinge that fills the gap.

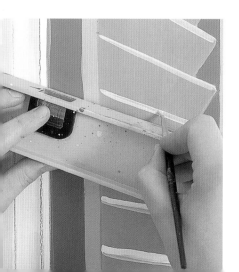

VARIATION 1 ▲▲▲

Louver doors are an appropriate opening to almost any kind of landscape, and can be painted whatever color complements the landscape or a room's interior.

FINISH ▲▲▲

This is a very methodical element, but the end result is worthwhile so stick with it.

VARIATION 2 ▶▶▶

The same principles and techniques used for a louver door have been applied to create this, seemingly very different, Chinese-style door.

PROJECTS

THE SIX PROJECTS FEATURED IN THIS MAIN SECTION OF THE BOOK ARE JUST A SMALL SAMPLE OF TROMPE

L'OEIL INTERIOR MURALS. THEY PROGRESS FROM RELATIVELY SIMPLE TO SLIGHTLY MORE COMPLICATED

DESIGNS, EACH ONE INCORPORATING AT LEAST ONE OF THE ELEMENTS FROM THE PREVIOUS CHAPTER. AS

YOU BECOME MORE CONFIDENT, YOU MIGHT DECIDE TO MIX AND MATCH DIFFERENT ELEMENTS WITH

OTHER FEATURES IN THESE PROJECTS TO MAKE YOUR OWN DESIGN. IN MY MANY YEARS IN THIS

PROFESSION, I HAVE SELDOM PAINTED THE SAME MURAL TWICE, YET MY PROCEDURES AND TECHNIQUES

GENERALLY REMAIN CONSTANT THROUGHOUT ALL OF THE MURALS.

SKY CEILING
WITH FOLIAGE

BACKGROUND

BUTTERFLY

The butterfly provides the opportunity to add vibrant colors to the mural on a small scale, at the same time giving it a focus point. This image can be used as a template.

PAINTING A CEILING MAY SEEM A DAUNTING PROSPECT, BUT DON'T BE PUT OFF. THIS SIMPLE MURAL IS AN IDEAL PROJECT TO START WITH; IT IS REASONABLY EASY TO EXECUTE, AND, INDEED, ALMOST SEEMS TO HAPPEN BY ITSELF, WITH MINIMUM EFFORT ON YOUR PART. THE WORK YOU DO PUT IN WILL BE AMPLY REWARDED. THE SOFT TONES CREATE A RELAXING ATMOSPHERE AND RAISE THE SPIRITS ON GRAY, OVERCAST DAYS. IN THIS PROJECT THE WALLS HAVE BEEN GIVEN A STONE BLOCKING EFFECT, BUT A SKY CEILING WILL LOOK GOOD EVEN ON ITS OWN.

COLOR PALETTE

Pure White

Raw Umber

Cobalt Blue

Mars Black

Chromium Oxide Green

Raw Sienna

Yellow Ochre

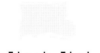

Flesh Tint

CHOOSING A SITE

Placing this mural in a bedroom enables you to view the painted sky from the ideal position—lying down. A bathroom also makes a good location, particularly for those who take baths rather than showers. The mural requires a flat ceiling, and ideally is free of light fittings so that the sky creates an impression of space—a hanging light will spoil the illusion by reminding the viewer of the ceiling's existence. Height is another important consideration. Bear in mind that unless you are lying flat, ceilings are seen from an angle, so the higher the ceiling is the more chance you have to crane your neck and view the mural almost face on.

STEP
BY STEP

STEP 1 ◀ ◀ ◀

The best way to carry out the painting is to stand on a step ladder; lying on your back on a scaffold restricts freedom of movement. Using Pure White and Cobalt Blue in varying proportions, mix up two or three shades of light blue in large plastic pots, adding about 6–8 parts water. Don't worry if the blue looks too light, as the effect is achieved by gradually intensifying the color as you work. Starting from the middle, paint the whole ceiling light blue using a large decorator's brush. Brush the paint in all directions, trying not to leave any obvious brushmarks. Repeat the process two or three times, letting the paint dry between coats. The result will be a very faint patchy blue. Gradually build up the depth of color with the darker blues, keeping these to the center of the ceiling, blending them out to the edges, and bringing in deeper blues as necessary. Think of the sky as one large cloud in which you are "punching holes" with the blues to let the clear sky show through.

STEP 2 ▶ ▶ ▶

When you start to see some cloud formations emerging, add some highlights to them using a smaller decorator's brush and Pure White mixed with about 3 parts water, then leave to dry. Mix Pure White with a little Flesh Tint and about 6–8 parts water, and wash this right over the cloud areas. This layer of thin color will modify the original blues to produce a very subtle pinkish gray, giving the clouds more form. Avoid becoming too involved with detail; the clouds should only be loosely suggested. Simplicity is the key to this effect; fussy detail would draw the eye to specific areas rather than encourage it to take in the ceiling as a whole.

STEP 3 ◀ ◀ ◀

Paint stone blocking on the walls following the steps in Stone Blocking (pages 46–49). Mix up a variety of greens using Pure White, Chromium Oxide Green, Yellow Ochre, and Mars Black. With two of the darker greens and a ⅝-inch (16mm) flat brush, paint in some random foliage around the top of the stone blocking, letting the brushmarks suggest simple leaf shapes (see Greenery, pages 64–69). Keep the greens darkest against the edges of the blocking, and carry some foliage down in a few random strands. With Raw Umber and a ⅜-inch (10mm) flat brush, paint overhanging strands of foliage curving in and out around the top of the wall.

STEP 4 ▶ ▶ ▶

Use the lighter greens to paint more foliage around the dark greens—this will appear to be higher up and catching more light. Complete the foliage effect by using the mid-tone mortar color and the ⅜-inch (10mm) flat brush to add some cast shadows under the leaves and branches.

STEP 5 ◀ ◀ ◀

For the final touch, paint a butterfly on the stone blocking. Use the template provided on page 76 or draw the shape from a reference of your own. Transfer the butterfly shape to the wall using semi-transparent transfer paper (see pages 34–35).

STEP 6 ▶ ▶ ▶

Using the mid-tone mortar color and a No. 3 round brush, paint in the outline of the butterfly. Use a ¼-inch (6mm) flat brush and the same color to add a cast shadow at the right and bottom, corresponding to the light source at upper left.

STEP 7 ◀ ◀ ◀

Build up the coloring of the butterfly gradually, first blocking in the larger areas of color and then adding the detailing with a finer brush. You can choose your colors according to a particular species of butterfly, but in this example I have used vibrant mixtures of Pure White and Cobalt Blue because they contrast well with the warm ochers of the stone blocking.

VARIATIONS

SKY EFFECTS
PASSING CLOUDS

◀ ◀ ◀

VARIATION 1

A decorative and slightly crumbling sandstone edge lends a softer line to the meeting of the wall and sky/ceiling.

▶ ▶ ▶

VARIATION 2

Technically not a sky ceiling, this mural was painted toward the vertex of a high wall, so the viewer looks up to see it. Notice that clouds appear different when viewed from an angle rather than directly above.

TEDDY BEAR
IN WINDOW

BACKGROUND

TEDDY

The teddy shape printed behind the type can be photocopied and used as a template for the teddy on the windowsill.

GENERALLY A MURAL STAYS WHERE IT HAS BEEN PAINTED UNTIL IT IS COVERED UP, WORN AWAY, OR DESTROYED. AN ALTERNATIVE IS TO PAINT YOUR MURAL ON A PANEL OF SOME KIND—EITHER CANVAS OR MEDIUM-DENSITY FIBERBOARD (MDF). THIS MEANS YOU CAN TAKE YOUR MURAL WITH YOU IN THE EVENT OF MOVING HOUSE, OR MOVE IT TO ANOTHER ROOM. PANELS OFFER ANOTHER ADVANTAGE—YOU CAN ACTUALLY PAINT YOUR MURAL ANYWHERE YOU LIKE, WHICH IS PARTICULARLY USEFUL WHEN SMALL CHILDREN ARE ABOUT. YOU CAN KEEP LITTLE ONES OUT OF YOUR PAINT POTS WHILE YOU WORK, AND PREVENT BUDDING YOUNG ARTISTS FROM IMPROVING ON YOUR MASTERPIECE WHILE YOU ARE OUT OF THE ROOM!

CHOOSING A SITE

Painting on canvas or MDF boards allows you to change your mural's position, but this is still limited by other circumstances such as light. You need to choose the place for your panel so that you know where the light source is. If you decide later to move your mural, the light source should be similar.

Although this is a child's mural, and children have lower eye levels than adults, the window should still be sited at a similar height to any real windows in the room, or the inconsistency will appear strange.

FINDING VISUAL REFERENCE

There are endless possibilities for a child's mural, and the most obvious place to find inspiration is from your children themselves. What are their favorite toys? Who is their favorite storybook character? The teddy in this mural appears to be a budding artist, reflecting my own interests, but you might consider giving yours a similar personal touch, relating to the child's own enthusiasms.

COLOR PALETTE

Medium Green latex (emulsion)

Raw Sienna

Pure White

Cadmium Orange

Chromium Oxide Green

Red Oxide

Cobalt Blue

Payne's Grey

Raw Umber

Mars Black

Yellow Ochre

PREPARATION

Have a piece of ½-inch (12mm) MDF cut to the size of 4 foot x 2 foot 9 inches (1.22m x 84cm) or thereabouts, then rub down the surface with fine sandpaper to the give it a key. To prime the board, lay on successive coats of acrylic primer or ordinary white latex (emulsion) paint. Allow each coat to dry, and sand the surface before applying the next. To ensure a smooth surface with no hairs trapped in the paint, use a good-quality decorator's brush or a paint roller; I often use a hog-hair varnishing brush. Leave the edges unprimed at this stage, as the panel will be cut down later. Leave to dry fully before proceeding.

STEP BY STEP

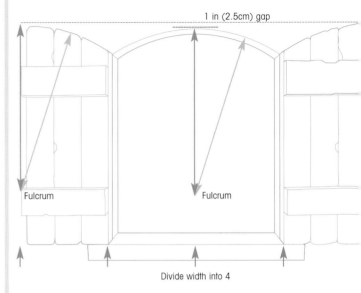

STEP 1 ▲▲▲

Divide the width into four to provide the basic framework. Follow the method on page 92 (step 1) to draw the window and door arches, using the points marked on the diagram as the fulcrums. Make sure you leave a gap of about 1 inch (2.5cm) between the top of the window and the top of the panel. The door fulcrums are about 1 inch (2.5cm) higher than the window fulcrum, so the top of each door should meet the top of the panel.

STEP 2 ▲▲▲

You may need to find someone to help cut out the MDF panel. Wear a mask over your nose and mouth to protect you from the MDF dust particles. Hold the panel firmly in place and cut around the outside edges of the design with a jigsaw. Take the saw slightly into the grooves between the planks and around all the variations in the line. When finished, sand the edges thoroughly, and prime (see page 24).

STEP 3 ▶ ▶ ▶

You can paint with the panel in a propped-up position, but fixing it flush to the wall is preferable; if the board is propped at an angle, paint drips may land on the painting rather than on the drop sheets. If fixings are put through the horizontal planks of the doors they will not look out of place. On the finished painting (page 83) you will see that there are six painted nails on each of the horizontal planks—on each door one of these is a real fixing. Place the fixings as close to the corners as aesthetics allow. With a ruler and charcoal pencil draw in the hinges. They should correspond with the horizontal panels and be drawn at a slant.

STEP 4 ◀ ◀ ◀

Transfer your teddy picture (see pages 34–35), and paint in all the outlines using a No. 3 round brush and Red Oxide mixed with a little water. When dry, block in the doors and the cut edges with the Medium Green mixed with about one part water. You will need a good-quality small decorator's brush—I am using a 1-inch (25mm) hog-hair brush. Build up two or three thin coats, letting the paint dry between each one. Don't worry about getting a completely even coat—a patchy look will add character. The Red Oxide lines should still be visible.

STEP 5 ▶ ▶ ▶

Make up a deeper green by mixing Red Oxide thinned with a little water into the green latex (emulsion), and use a No. 5 round brush to paint a thicker outline. Use the same color to paint a thick shadow beneath the horizontal planks (the tops will be highlighted). As the light source is at upper left, the right edge of the right-hand door is slightly in shadow and is painted a deeper green. Paint a shadow line at the bottom of each door and flick or dab in some lines at the bottoms and tops, and add a few holes here and there to create the impression of old woodwork. Paint in more nail- or screw-heads on the horizontal planks to help disguise the real ones. These are simply a blob of deep green with a highlight.

STEP 6 ▶ ▶ ▶

Mix up a darker green by adding a little black to the green that was used in step 5. To give the impression of the deep grooves between the planks, use a No. 3 round brush and a level to paint a finer line in the middle of the thick, deep green line. Also use this dark color to emphasize any holes and wood splits and to pick out a few finer details. Make a light green by adding Pure White to the Medium Green, and pick out the highlights on the windows with Nos. 3 and 5 round brushes. Highlight the top edges of the horizontal panels and the inside edges where the hinges are.

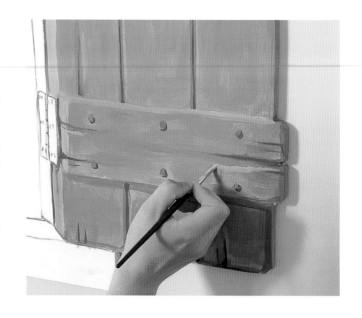

STEP 7 ◀ ◀ ◀

Using a ⅝-inch (16mm) flat brush, paint the windowsill with Raw Sienna mixed with Pure White, then use a lighter mix on the top of the sill and around the left, right, and top edges of the window. Mix in some Raw Umber and paint some shadows beneath the teddy with a ⅜-inch (10mm) flat brush.

STEP 8 ▶ ▶ ▶

In separate pots, mix up three or four blues ranging from light to dark, using varying quantities of Cobalt Blue and Pure White mixed with about one part water each. Paint the sky from the top down, beginning with the dark blue, cutting it in neatly under the arch of the window, and then gradually blending the blues from dark to light as you work down to the windowsill. The first coat will look patchy, but don't worry; let the paint dry and repeat the process until you have a solid layer of blues.

STEP 9 ▶ ▶ ▶

Paint in some clouds using the palest sky-blue color and a ⅝-inch (16mm) flat brush or a 1-inch (25mm) hog-hair varnishing brush. You may need to water the color down slightly. Paint in the tops of the clouds first and then blend the color downward, perhaps using some water to fade the color out. This will give a more defined cloud edge at the top. Leave this to dry. Paint another cloud area just below the first to give the impression of clouds overlapping each other—you want to avoid the cotton cloud effect. As you work down toward the windowsill, use Pure White for the clouds to make them stand out against the paler blue. Add some finer highlights with a ⅜-inch (10mm) flat brush.

STEP 10 ▲ ▲ ▲

Paint the hinges with a ⅜-inch (10mm) flat brush, using the deep sky blue and then adding some Raw Umber to build up the metal color. Pick out the details with a No. 1 round brush and a dark mixture of Cobalt Blue and Raw Umber, then add some Pure White highlights with the same brush.

STEP 11 ▶ ▶ ▶

Block in the teddy with a ⅝-inch (16mm) flat brush and a mixture of Raw Sienna and Pure White, pushing the paint with the end of the brush to suggest the furry texture. Add more Raw Umber for the shadows, and use this darker color to pick out the facial details, joints, and stitches.

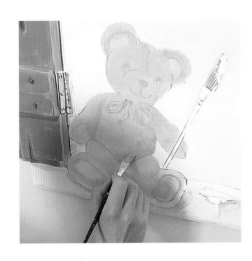

STEP 12 ▲ ▲ ▲

Build up the detailing, painting the paw pads with Raw Umber mixed with Yellow Ochre and Pure White, and then paint the bow with Red Oxide and a ¼-inch (6mm) flat brush. Add some Chromium Oxide Green to the Red Oxide to make a deeper red for the shadows in the bow, and then paint the cast shadows on the teddy's body with the color used for the paw pads.

STEP 13 ▶ ▶ ▶

Add further touches of detail to the teddy with Nos. 1 and 3 round brushes before blocking in the blob of green paint, starting with the Medium Green latex (emulsion) and then picking out the lowlights and highlights in the respective green mixes. Paint the brush by first blocking it in with a mix of Yellow Ochre, Raw Umber, and Pure White, and then hint at the individual bristles with strokes of Raw Umber. Add a shadow to the bristles where they meet the blob of green paint. Suggest the form of the brush's metal ferrule with varied mixes of Pure White and Payne's Grey, using Pure White alone to add a single line of highlight.

STEP 14 ◀ ◀ ◀

Paint the blob of paint on the windowsill in the same way as the one on the teddy's brush, then add some highlights and lowlights on the paw pads using the No. 3 round brush. Add Pure White to the paw-pad mixture for the highlights, and more Raw Umber for the lowlights. Here the light comes from the left, so the highlights are at the top left of the pads and the lowlights at the bottom right edge.

STEP 15 ▶ ▶ ▶

Use a No. 3 round brush to complete the teddy's eyes. First block them in with Cadmium Orange, then allow to dry and paint the black pupils. Finally, add a small blob of Pure White to each eye to make a sharp highlight.

VARIATIONS

CHILD'S
BEDROOM

VARIATION 1

The toy box and shelf is a relatively simple trompe l'oeil to paint, as there is no need to place them within a "frame," such as a niche, window, or doorway, and no background is required other than the wall itself.

VARIATION 2

By the time children have outgrown their teddy bears and toys, they are probably dreaming of what they will be when they grow up; a ballerina, an astronaut, or perhaps a race car driver.

STONE URN
IN NICHE WITH CURTAIN

STONE URN

The stone urn shape printed behind the type can be photocopied and used as a template for your mural.

SINCE CLASSICAL TIMES, STONE AND CERAMIC URNS HAVE BEEN USED TO CREATE FOCAL POINTS IN GARDENS AND INTERIORS. URNS CAN ACCENTUATE ARCHITECTURAL FEATURES, ADD VISUAL VARIETY TO LONG BALUSTRADES, AND DRAW THE EYE ALONG CORRIDORS OR FORMAL GARDEN PATHS, WHILE OPEN-TOPPED URNS CAN BE TURNED INTO COLORFUL CONTAINERS FILLED WITH EITHER CUT FLOWERS OR LIVING PLANTS.

In this project, a niche provides the architectural context for the urn, and a curtain softens the austere lines and provides a contrast of both color and texture. You can vary and personalize a feature of this kind, perhaps by adding a bird, flowers, or a decorative design to the curtain—this might match an existing fabric in the room where the mural is painted.

CHOOSING A SITE

The choice of site is vital for any trompe l'oeil mural, but is especially so for this feature, as its success largely depends on where it is placed. Make it a focal point at the top of a landing or at the end of a hallway, or paint a pair of niches flanking a fireplace or entranceway.

The niche should be in proportion to the other architectural features in the room, including fireplaces, moldings, and windows. The size of the urn is obviously determined by that of the niche, or vice versa, but you must consider the proportion of urn to niche. To fit comfortably in its place the urn should be half as wide as the niche and roughly half as tall. The top of the urn should be at about eye level so that the top ellipse is almost straight, and the bottom one, where the urn joins the pedestal, forms a gentle curve. Ellipses become progressively wider open the farther they are below eye level.

FINDING VISUAL REFERENCE

Urns vary widely in their degree and style of ornamentation, from classical simplicity to the extravagance of the Baroque and Rococo, so take the time to look through books and brochures to collect visual references—if possible also try to obtain the dimensions. Bear in mind that an urn with a lot of surface ornamentation will be harder to paint, as the patterns will be distorted by the curve of the surface, so if this is your first attempt it would be wise to err on the side of caution and choose a relatively plain urn.

COLOR PALETTE

Pure White

Raw Umber

Burnt Sienna

Payne's Grey

Yellow Ochre

Cobalt Blue

Flesh Tint

Gold (for the tie-back)

STEP BY STEP

STEP 1 ▲▲▲

Having planned out the dimensions of your niche and urn, draw the niche onto the wall. Using a charcoal pencil and a large level, first draw in a vertical line to determine the center of the niche and the center line for the urn. Draw in the sides at equal distances from the center vertical, and then the bottom of the niche, remembering that the width of the niche should be around twice that of the urn.

To draw an arc in the niche, tie a piece of string onto the charcoal pencil, near the tip, and hold it at this center point—the fulcrum—then stretch the other end so that it touches the vertical edge of the niche. Hold this end firmly and push the pencil around slowly to draw in the top semicircle, keeping the string taut and the pencil steady and at a right angle to the surface of the wall.

STEP 2 ▼▼▼

Draw your urn with a graphite pencil on a piece of tracing or transfer paper—or kitchen wax paper, which is what I have used. Because urns are symmetrical you will only need to plan out half of it. Transfer the design as usual (see pages 34–35).

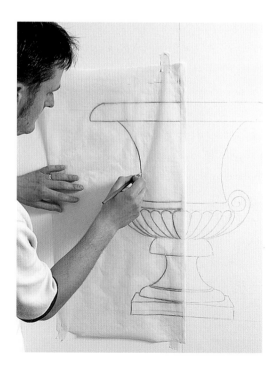

STEP 3

Refer to the Drape element on pages 50–53, and draw in the curtain and tie-back. Add a curtain pole on the wall above the niche. The rail should be longer than the width of the niche, with the curtain hanging from it by loops. Mix some Payne's Grey and Pure White with about one part water. (This will be the shadow tone.) Paint over all the charcoal outlines using Nos. 3 and 5 round brushes. Use the smaller brush for the finer outlining on the urn.

STEP 4 ▶ ▶ ▶

For the urn's base tone, mix a lot of Pure White, Flesh Tint, and Cobalt Blue, and gradually add about five parts water. Paint in the color quite freely, not worrying too much about going over the edges. The outline should still be visible. Mix a medium base color wash for the niche and wall in a large plastic pot, using Pure White, Yellow Ochre, and Raw Umber. Gradually mix in about six parts water. With a large decorator's brush, paint the wall outside the niche to give a stony look.

STEP 5 ▶ ▶ ▶

Mix a mid tone using the same colors but with less Pure White and more Raw Umber, and for a dark tone increase the proportion of Raw Umber even more, mixing the color in a smaller pot with a small quantity of water. Add shadows on the wall to the left of the curtain and under the sill using the darkest shadow tone and the ⅝-inch (16mm) flat brush. Block in the niche area, using both the base tone and the mid tone. Use a ⅝-inch (16mm) flat brush to cut in around the edges of the niche and urn, and a larger decorator's brush for the less intricate areas. The light source in this case is at upper right, so you will need to use the mid tone for the right-hand side and top edge of the niche, blending this into the base tone about halfway into it. Use the mid tone also to the left of the urn to indicate the cast shadow, then define the deeper shadows— along the right-hand and top edges of the niche and at the base to the left of the urn— using the dark tone.

STEP 6 ▶ ▶ ▶

For the curtain's base color, mix Pure White, a little Cobalt Blue, and Burnt Sienna, to about four parts water. With a small decorator's brush block in the curtain, and use the ⅝-inch (16mm) flat brush to paint up to the edges.

Holding a level against the wall, paint a cast shadow beneath the curtain pole with the shadow tone mixed in step 3. Here, the shadow from the ball-shaped finials will be below to the left. Add a small diagonal shadow near each end to indicate the fixing that holds the pole up, or the pole will appear to be floating in front of the wall. Add shading and highlights to the curtain (see Drape, page 52).

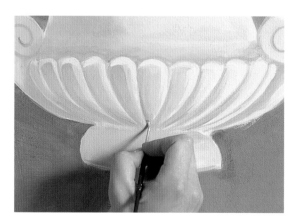

STEP 7 ◀ ◀ ◀

Mix two deeper tones for the urn, using the base tone colors but with the addition of Payne's Grey. Vary the proportions so that the mid tone is pinkish, and the other more blue. Begin modeling the urn with these new tones, building up the main areas of shadow gradually and blending them into the base tone. Start with the ⅝-inch (16mm) flat brush, switching to a smaller flat brush for any intricate areas such as the detailing around the fluting. Always keep the light source in mind so that you can make the play of light and shadow logical. Add shadows under the lip of the urn, on the fluting, and on the detailing of the urn, using them to suggest the curvature of the urn's surface. The left-hand side is mainly in shadow, but there is a small band of reflected light on the edge, so lighten the tone slightly to enhance the curvature effect.

STEP 8 ▲ ▲ ▲

Make a darker tone for the fine detailing by mixing a little Pure White with some Payne's Grey, Raw Umber, and just a little water. Using Nos. 1 and 3 round brushes, work the color into the grooves in the fluting and the detailing on the handles. The color should be blended into the others to avoid a hard cutout effect, so have some of the earlier colors on hand.

STEP 9 ▲ ▲ ▲

Load a ¼-inch (6mm) flat brush with Gold, and paint the tie-back and tassel using a series of S-shaped brushstrokes. To define the shadows and detailing, use a No. 1 or 3 round brush, mixing some Raw Umber into the Gold.

VARIATIONS

URNS

VARIATION 1

This aged and weathered sandstone urn is brought into the present by the addition of the celebratory champagne and glasses, and is used, somewhat irreverently, as an ice bucket!

VARIATION 2

The classical urn has been replaced by an ancient Greek vase depicting scenes from myth and legend, placed atop a pedestal.

STONE ARCHWAY
& CLASSICAL GARDEN

TEMPLE

The image printed behind the type can be copied, scaled appropriately, and used as a template. In this project the temple is about 10¼ inches (26cm) high.

FEW OF US WOULD HAVE THE SPACE OR MEANS TO OWN SUCH A GARDEN AS THIS, OR, INDEED, THE PATIENCE TO CULTIVATE AND MAINTAIN IT. THE MURAL'S EFFECTIVENESS RELIES LARGELY ON THE USE OF PERSPECTIVE. THE LONG LINES OF THE YARD, POND, AND HEDGES DRAW THE EYE OUT OF THE ROOM TO FOCUS ON THE CLASSICAL TEMPLE, THE FORMAL SYMMETRY OF THE SCENE SOFTENED JUST A LITTLE BY THE VARIATION IN THE DISTANT TREES AND FOLIAGE BEYOND. INFLUENCED BY THE GARDENS OF GRAND ITALIAN COUNTRY MANSIONS AND PALACES, THE SCENE IS AT ONCE FORMAL AND CALMING.

CHOOSING A SITE

This mural would be suited to a variety of locations, but it is important to be able to view it from a reasonable distance so that its full height can be seen. The end of a formal hallway would be an excellent site, in keeping with the character of the mural. The stone blocking can, of course, be carried along the rest of the walls to unite the space, and the mural could be enhanced by placing a pair of small topiary trees or something similar—either real or painted—on either side of the archway. I have painted a similar mural with a classical temple in the relaxation room of a health spa, making an obvious link with the Romans, who placed great value on the pursuit of bodily and spiritual health.

FINDING VISUAL REFERENCE

Templates for the temple and balustrade (page 54) have been provided, but you may wish to use different architectural features, or work with the details to produce a different look or style. There is no shortage of books available on architecture through history, and flicking through one is bound to provide ample inspiration. Do make sure, however, that the different architectural elements you choose complement each other in terms of style and period.

COLOR PALETTE

Flesh Tint

Cobalt Blue

Payne's Grey

Chromium Oxide Green

Yellow Ochre

Sap Green

Mars Black

Burnt Sienna

Pure White

STEP
BY STEP

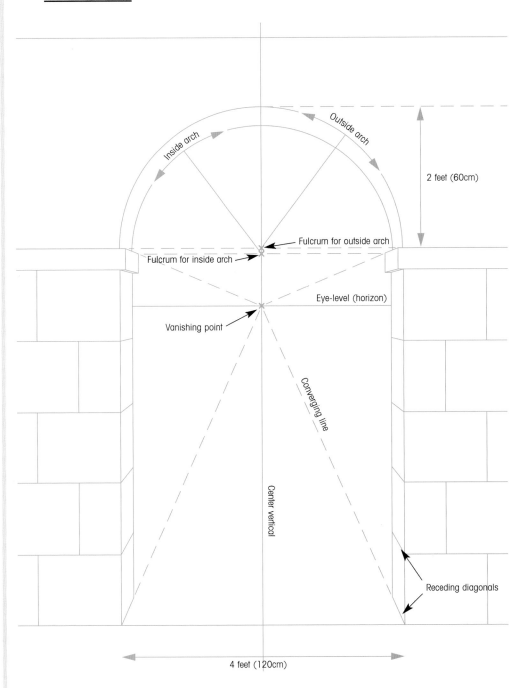

STEP 1 ▲▲▲

Follow the diagram to work out the proportions of the archway and the perspective of the stone blocking; use a level for the vertical and horizontal lines, and the string and pencil method for the receding diagonals with the string fixed at the vanishing point (see Perspective, pages 36–39). You can change the measurements if you wish, but plan out the arch on paper first. Note that there should be a reasonable gap between the top of the arch and the top of the wall, and that the width of the opening will determine the size of the arch. To draw the outer and inner arches, follow the method explained on page 92 (step 1), using the two points marked on the diagram as the fulcrums.

STEP 2 ▼▼▼

Mark in the bottom of the balustrading by drawing a horizontal line about 15 inches (38cm) up from the bottom of the mural, then transfer your baluster design (see pages 34–35). Note that, because they are set back a little, the balustrades are smaller than life size. Here the balusters are approximately 18½ inches (43cm) tall.

STEP 3 ▶▶▶

In a plastic pot, mix up a mid-tone stone color using Flesh Tint, Cobalt Blue, and a little Pure White with water. Using a ¼-inch (6mm) flat brush, paint in the mortar lines for the stone blocking, using a level as a guide for the straight lines. Paint the rest of the arch outline in the same color, this time with a No. 3 round brush.

STEP 4 ▶▶▶

The gap between the bottom of the balustrading and the bottom of the wall represents the paved area, which is a rectangular shape seen in perspective. Using the string fixed at the vanishing point, paint two lines converging inward from each side of the opening, then divide the area into three foreshortened sections by using the simple geometric technique described on page 39.

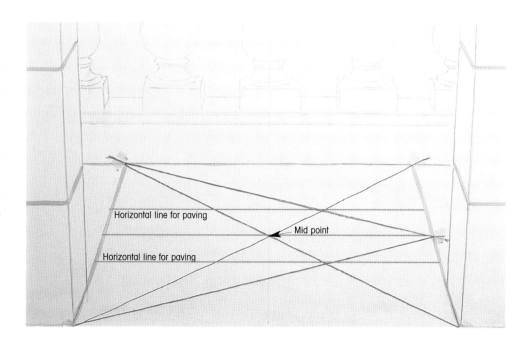

Horizontal line for paving

Mid point

Horizontal line for paving

STEP 5 ▼ ▼ ▼

Work out the converging perspective lines of the paving stones by dividing the width of the opening at the bottom by three and then use the string and vanishing point to mark them in. Paint in the outlines of the balustrading using a No. 3 round brush and the mid-tone stone color.

STEP 6 ▲ ▲ ▲

Scale up your temple image (see pages 32-33). The temple is about 10¼ inches (26cm) high. Transfer the image to the wall (see pages 34–35), positioning it so that the center vertical of the temple lines up with the center vertical on the wall, with the eye level line on the wall about a third of the way up the height of the temple. Paint in the outline with the mid-tone stone color and Nos. 1 and 3 round brushes.

STEP 7 ▶ ▶ ▶

Use the level to draw the horizontals of the pond, and the string for the perspective lines at left and right (see diagram on page 37). Make sure that the design is symmetrical by checking the measurements on each side. Paint the outlines as before, with a No. 3 round brush.

Using a level, plan out a simple hedge on each side of the temple, about half its height, then use the string fixed at the vanishing point to draw the sides seen in perspective—these give the impression that the hedge encloses the entire garden. Using the same color and brush, sketch in the outlines.

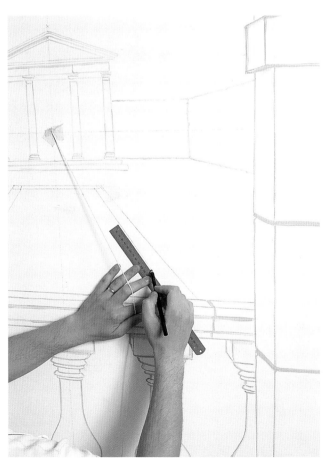

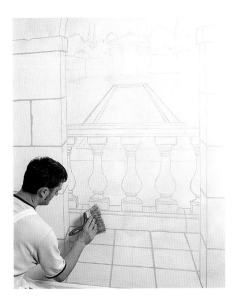

STEP 8 ▲▲▲

In a large plastic pot, make up a color wash using Flesh Tint and Cobalt Blue mixed with a larger quantity of Pure White and about 15–20 parts water. This is the base color for the whole of the mural, so paint it all over the surface using a large decorator's brush and working in all directions. Make sure to catch any drips as you work, and repeat the process two or three times. Let the paint dry thoroughly between each coat.

STEP 9 ▲▲▲

Mix up three or four light to dark blues using varying quantities of Cobalt Blue and Pure White with a little water. Mark the plastic pots with a marker pen so that you know the order of colors. Starting with the deepest blue, and using a 1-inch (25mm) brush and a ⅝-inch (16mm) flat brush, cut in around the top of the archway and then paint downward, gradually blending the blues from dark to light. To achieve smooth gradations of color, repeat the process a few times. To add some clouds, follow steps 8–9 of Teddy Bear in Window, pages 86–87.

STEP 10 ▶▶▶

For the background foliage, mix up three greens ranging from light to dark using varying quantities of Cobalt Blue, Chromium Oxide Green, and Pure White, with a little water. Label the pots, then loosely block in the trees using the mid tone and the ⅝-inch (16mm) flat brush. Aim for a slightly patchy effect to describe the foliage texture. For the hedge, you will need several different greens based on mixtures of Chromium Oxide Green, Yellow Ochre, and Pure White. To make a darker green, use more Chromium Oxide Green and Mars Black, and for the lightest

one use more white and no black. The mid green should be halfway between the two. Block in the hedge using the ⅝-inch (16mm) flat brush, paying attention to the light source—here the upper left, so the hedge on the left is painted in the darker green stippled with a little mid green. The area on each side of the temple is stippled with the mid green with a little of the dark green, and the right-hand hedge is stippled with the light green with a little of the mid green.

STEP 11 ▼▼▼

Mix up two or three greens for the grass, using Chromium Oxide Green, Yellow Ochre, Sap Green, and Pure White with a little water. Using a 1-inch (2.5cm) hog-hair brush or similar and a ⅝-inch (16mm) brush, block in the area, including the spaces between the balusters. To give slight variations in tone, dip the brush into two or more of the colors at the same time so that they mix partially—if you use one color alone the grass will look flat and lifeless. Also try stippling in places to vary the effect.

STEP 12 ▲▲▲

Now add some clouds to the sky using a ⅜-inch (10mm) flat brush and the lightest blue (see page 101, step 9) mixed with Pure White. Mix a wash of Pure White and Flesh Tint and brush a little of this into some of the clouds to add further color. Return to the background foliage and the colors mixed in step 11. Using a ⅜-inch (10mm) flat brush, stipple and smudge in a dark area, blending it into the mid green. Then stipple below this area with the light green to give the impression of different layers of trees and bushes. Darken the cypress trees, especially at the base, and again stipple some of the lighter green underneath. Blend the mid green into the dark where the trees meet the top of the hedges, and deepen the greens where they meet the edges of the temple.

STEP 13 ▶▶▶

To achieve the correct perspective for the cast shadow by the left-hand hedge, attach the string at the vanishing point and mark in the line, then paint the shadow with the ⅜-inch (10mm) flat brush, using one of the darker grass colors mixed with a little black. Paint the diagonal shadow on the hedge with the dark hedge green, and deepen the color of the hedge at the base and to the right of the temple. Stipple in a highlight at the top of the hedge with the lightest hedge color.

STEP 14 ▶▶▶

Now start to work on the temple, starting with the ¼-inch (6mm) flat brush and the mid-tone stone color. Mix a little Payne's Grey into some of this to make a deeper color, and add some shadows around the architectural moldings and a cast shadow on the back wall of the temple. Give a simple stone blocking effect (see pages 46–49) to the back wall of the temple, using a No. 1 round brush. (I have included a simplified mini-version of the Stone Urn in Niche project, pages 90–95, but this, of course, is optional.) Mix a lighter stone color by adding white to the mid tone, and pick out the highlights on the portico and column moldings.

STEP 15 ▶▶▶

Work out the sizes of the paving slabs around the pond using the technique on page 39, then mix up a mid-tone pond color using Cobalt Blue, Chromium Oxide Green, Burnt Sienna, and Pure White with a little water. For a lighter tone, add more white and blue, and add black for the dark tone. Using the middle and light tones and a ⅝-inch (16mm) flat brush, paint in the pond surface with horizontal brushstrokes. Suggest the reflection of the paving stones around the pond edges with the mid tone.

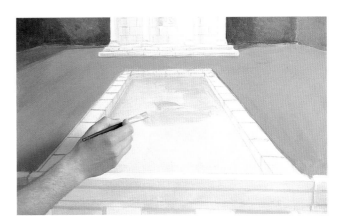

STEP 16 ▶▶▶

Using the colors mixed for the temple, bring the balustrading to near-completion following steps 4–7 of the Balustrading element (pages 56–57). Now to the paving slabs of the patio. Paint the cast shadow at the top of the slabs using the mid-tone stone color mixed with the original background color wash. This shadow gives the impression that the sun is high in the sky—if it were lower, each of the balusters would cast their own shadow. Define the mortar lines in the paving using the dark stone color and a No. 3 round brush, then paint highlights and lowlights, using all the stone colors, and adding a few cracks and chips here and there.

STEP 17

Gradually deepen the greens between the balusters to emphasize their shape, and follow Greenery (page 66, steps 3–5) to build up a simple foliage effect. Slightly deepen the greens around the edges of the pond and add stray grasses here and there with small round brushstrokes.

STEP 18 ◀ ◀ ◀

Measure the top edge of the pond, divide this figure by three, and make corresponding marks along the edge of the pond. Mark these same measurements across the lawn on both sides of the pond, then again attach the string to the vanishing point, align it with each mark and faintly draw in the converging perspective lines. Mix a lighter shade of green by adding Pure White to one of the grass colors, and paint in each stripe with the ⅝-inch (16mm) flat brush. Stipple in some moss in the gaps and around the paving slabs with the ⅜-inch (10mm) flat brush and any of the deeper greens.

STEP 19 ▼ ▼ ▼

To work out the reflections, use the temple design image from step 6, turning it upside down and positioning it as shown, with a gap of about ⅜ inch (10mm) between the temple and its reflection. Make sure that it is level before transferring the image onto the mural. Loosely paint in the outline with the mid-tone pond color mixed in step 15, slightly distorting the line to give the effect of a rippling water surface.

STEP 20 ▲ ▲ ▲

Using the three pond colors and the stone colors, gradually build up the shapes of the reflections, using the two flat brushes and the No. 3 round brush. Take care with the perspective and shading. Note that the underside of the portico appears thicker in the reflection, as more of its underside is visible. If you have included the niche and urn, you can work out its position very simply by taking a measurement from the arch to the top of the wall on the actual temple and transferring this to the reflection. Define the columns in the lightest stone color to make them stand out well, and don't forget to distort the edges a little.

ARCHWAYS
AND GARDENS

VARIATION 1

The back drop to a luxurious pool room, three trompe l'oeil arches have been designed to incorporate a real window through which glimpses of real foliage can be seen.

VARIATION 2

Here a garden is viewed through two archways. The first extends the size of the actual room, and the second enhances the illusion of depth.

WESTERN
SCENE

COW SKULL & COWBOY

The images above and below can be used as templates should you wish to include these features in your design. In this mural, the cowboy sits about 4 inches (10cm) high, and the cow skull is slightly smaller than life size.

THE AMERICAN WEST CONTAINS SOME OF THE MOST BREATHTAKING LANDSCAPES IN THE WORLD, AND THE INSPIRATION FOR THIS MURAL WAS DRAWN FROM THE SPECTACULAR MEGALITHS AND OTHERWORLDLY LANDSCAPE OF MONUMENT VALLEY. AS THIS HAS BEEN A FAVORED LOCATION FOR FILMING WESTERNS, IT SEEMED APPROPRIATE—THOUGH PERHAPS RATHER A CLICHÉ—TO INCLUDE A SOLITARY COWBOY ON HORSEBACK SURVEYING THE SCENE FROM A ROCKY OUTCROP.

CHOOSING A SITE

Although unusual, this is a particularly versatile scene. As a landscape viewed through louver doors or a crumbling wall, it is a "serious" piece that could easily replace the more traditional Tuscan landscape. However it is tempting to include some of the colorful characters associated with the "Wild West," and their addition makes the mural ideal for a child's bedroom. You might decide to carry the theme across the entire wall, or even the whole room, and completely immerse the viewer in a make-believe world.

FINDING VISUAL REFERENCE

Since Monument Valley is among the most photographed landscapes in the world, it should not be hard to find suitable references. This is a relatively complex mural in which composition is a vital consideration, so I recommend first planning it out on paper in a concept sketch. To give the cowboy more prominence, I have placed him high up in the landscape and have ensured that he is not set against a complicated background. The greenery and water divide the back- and foreground, and the solitary cactus overlaps the water to form a link between the two main areas. The cracks in the foreground lead the eye in to give a feeling of depth, and the skull adds foreground interest as well as reinforcing the sense of place, reminding us that the beauty of the landscape co-exists with one of the most hostile climates in the world.

COLOR PALETTE

Pure White

Raw Umber

Burnt Sienna

Sap Green

Cobalt Blue

Yellow Ochre

Red Oxide

Chromium Oxide Green

Raw Sienna

Yellow Oxide

Dioxazine Purple

Mars Black

STEP
BY STEP

STEP 1 ▶ ▶ ▶

Plan the doorway frame. Faintly draw in a center vertical line using a level and a charcoal pencil, then decide on the width of the doorway opening and make two more faint verticals. Draw in a horizontal line, again using the level. These lines provide a guide for sketching out the opening. The measurements I have used are seen in the diagram. Draw the wooden supports freehand to give a natural line, and vary their thicknesses slightly to give a more rustic feel and to suggest occasional splits at the ends. Establish and mark the eye-level line. This crosses the center vertical at the vanishing point. Fix some string at this point and mark in the diagonal depth lines at each corner of the opening. Sketch in the inside lines of the opening, then paint in the outlines with a No. 5 round brush and Red Oxide mixed with a little water.

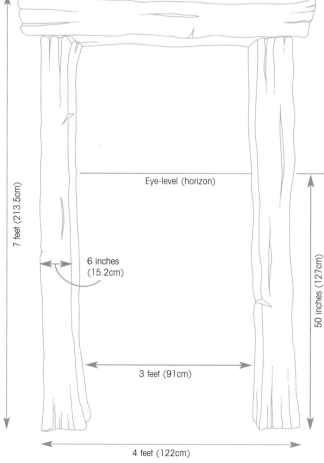

Eye-level (horizon)

7 feet (213.5cm)

6 inches (15.2cm)

50 inches (127cm)

3 feet (91cm)

4 feet (122cm)

STEP 2 ▼ ▼ ▼

Fix a sheet of semi-transparent transfer paper across the middle of the mural, and refer to your references and sketch, if you have made one, to plan out the background landscape. Just draw the basic shapes, standing back from time to time to get an overall

feel. The landscape here is built up in layers from the very distant monolith to the cactus in the foreground. I have sketched in the main monolith on the left very loosely, using the reference material only as a guide to the rock formations. Note how the lines of the monolith are almost vertical, spreading out at a shallow angle at the base, which should be placed on or near the eye-level line. Indicate some scattered foliage clinging to the base and going down to the water's edge, and copy other features you wish to include in the foreground, such as the cactus and skull. The cowboy will be left until the final stages.

STEP 3

Transfer the sketch onto the wall (see pages 34–35). Paint the outlines in Red Oxide, using Nos. 3 and 5 round brushes, then leave to dry.

STEP 4 ▶ ▶ ▶

In a large plastic pot, mix up a color wash using Pure White with Yellow Ochre and a little Raw Umber mixed with about 15 parts water. Lay three or four coats of this base color over the whole area with a large decorator's brush. Make sure the outlines are still visible, and let each coat dry before applying the next.

STEP 5 ◀ ◀ ◀

Using varying amounts of Cobalt Blue mixed with Pure White and a little water, make up three or four sky blues ranging from dark to light, then label each pot for reference. Start painting the sky from the top downward, working from dark at the top to light at the bottom. Use a ⅝-inch (16mm) flat brush for cutting in around the door frame and rocks, and a 1-inch (25mm) hog-hair brush or similar for blending. Repeat this a few times, letting the paint dry between coats, until you have a smooth gradation of color.

STEP 6 ▶ ▶ ▶

Mix two tones of purple in small plastic pots, using Dioxazine Purple and Pure White mixed with a little Cobalt Blue and water. Paint in the distant monolith and surroundings with the ⅝-inch (16mm) flat brush, varying the tones to suggest vague shadows and highlights and deepening the color where it meets the next layer of landscape.

STEP 7 ▲ ▲ ▲

Now begin to build up the middleground, for which you will need three more colors. Make a medium base color by mixing Burnt Sienna, Raw Umber, Pure White, and a little water. For the mid tone, add Cobalt Blue and use less white. For the deepest tone, use Burnt Sienna on its own mixed in with a little water. Label the pots as before. Using the ⅝-inch (16mm) flat brush, block in the large monolith and middleground with the medium base color, then paint in the large areas of shadow with the two darker tones. At the base of the monolith, make horizontal brushstrokes of the deeper color to suggest the craggy, stepped effect. At the same time, add shadows on the ground around the areas of foliage.

STEP 8 ▲ ▲ ▲

Mix two more browns, using Raw Sienna with 1–2 parts water for one, and Raw Sienna plus a little Pure White and water for the other. Freely block in the foreground around the cactus and skull with a small decorator's brush, darkening the color around the edges of the skull and the base of the cactus.

STEP 9 ▶ ▶ ▶

Mix up four or five different greens from Chromium Oxide Green, Yellow Ochre, Sap Green, Yellow Oxide, and Pure White. Make a darker green for the lowlights using a little Mars Black mixed with Chromium Oxide Green. Label the pots in order of tones from light to dark, then block in the foliage and the cactus with one of the mid tones and the ⅝-inch (16mm) flat brush. Use a ⅜-inch (10mm) flat brush to stipple in the light and dark greens (see Stone Archway & Classical Garden, pages 101–102, steps 10–12).

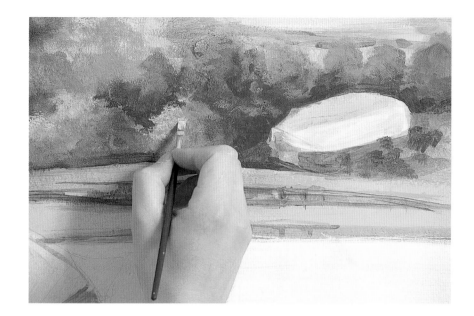

STEP 10 ▶ ▶ ▶

Using the Raw Sienna foreground color combined with the deep shadow tone used on the middleground (step 7), block in the doorway frame with a small decorator's brush or a 1-inch (25mm) hog-hair brush. Let the brushstrokes follow the direction of the wood to suggest the grain. Do not paint the inside of the frame, as this should be left lighter. Accentuate the wood splits and some of the grain with Raw Umber and a No. 3 round brush. Pick out some highlights using Pure White mixed with a little Raw Sienna.

STEP 11 ▲ ▲ ▲

To suggest a vague reflection in the water, use the middleground colors and some of the mid greens to paint horizontal strokes with the ⅝-inch (16mm) flat brush, then wash water over, and blend them together. Wash the pale middleground color into the greens in the upper areas of water and into the blues at the bottom. To give greater definition, wash in some of the deep middleground color at the very top edge where the water meets the dry land. Repeat the whole process until you are satisfied with the color gradations.

STEP 12 ▲ ▲ ▲

Using a ⅜-inch (10mm) flat brush, stipple some Pure White horizontal lines over the water to suggest rippling on the surface. Don't overdo this—you can always add a few more ripples later on if you wish.

STEP 13 ▶ ▶ ▶

Mix some Raw Umber with the darker foreground color to make a shadow tone, and use the ⅝-inch (16mm) flat brush to indicate some cast shadows to the right of the cactus (the light is coming from the left) and around the rocks and skull. With the same brush, paint some random cracking in the earth, holding the brush edge horizontal to the wall and making random zigzag patterns.

STEP 14 ▶ ▶ ▶

Using the foliage greens, add the cactus detail with a No. 5 round brush, keeping the light source in mind. Here the light comes from the left, so the cactus is slightly darker on the right-hand side. Paint in the ridges of the cactus using a darker green, and blend it into the lighter greens. Try not to make the ridges look like uniform stripes—if possible, have some reference material to hand.

STEP 15 ▼ ▼ ▼

Now paint the skull using the ⅝-inch (16mm) flat brush, starting with a mid tone mixed from Pure White, a little Cobalt Blue, and Burnt Sienna. With the same brush, work in some highlights and lowlights using Pure White for the former and Raw Umber smudged into the mid tone for the latter. To give the skull a grittier look, mix in some of the earth tones used to paint the landscape.

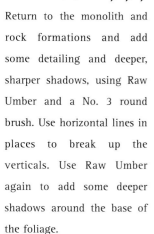

STEP 16 ▶ ▶ ▶

Return to the monolith and rock formations and add some detailing and deeper, sharper shadows, using Raw Umber and a No. 3 round brush. Use horizontal lines in places to break up the verticals. Use Raw Umber again to add some deeper shadows around the base of the foliage.

STEP 17 ▶▶▶

With the same color and brush, deepen the cracks in the foreground, then paint some linear highlights here and there using Pure White mixed with a little Raw Sienna. Add a few blades of grass growing out of the cracks with a No. 1 or 3 round brush and a dark green, flicking the brush upward to follow the direction of growth. Paint some paler blades over the dark ones using the same technique and a lighter green. Also add some grass around the base of the cactus, and around the skull if you wish.

STEP 18 ▶▶▶

And now for the final touch. Using the template provided (page 106), transfer the cowboy image onto semi-transparent transfer paper (see pages 34–35). Take care over the scale; the cowboy in this mural is about 4 inches (10cm) high. Transfer the image, then paint the outline with Raw Umber and a No. 1 round brush.

STEP 19 ◀◀◀

Build up the colors gradually. Start by blocking in the main areas, using Burnt Sienna and Raw Umber for the horse, and Raw Sienna and one of the sky blues for the cowboy. Pick out the finer detailing with a No. 1 round brush, but avoid too much detail, as the cowboy is in the middle distance. As you work, keep standing back from the mural to make sure that the level of detail is in keeping with that of the immediate surroundings.

VARIATIONS
COWBOYS
AND INDIANS

▶ ▶ ▶
VARIATION 1

This mural has been extended around each wall of a child's bedroom, not only creating a complete fantasy world, but replacing four cramped walls with boundless horizons.

◀ ◀ ◀
VARIATION 2

Part of the same mural, a couple of Indians approach the cowboy's camp. The open can of baked beans adds a special touch.

TUSCANY
WINDOW

WINE GLASS

This wine glass can be photocopied and used as a template. Alternatively, if you have a favorite set of wine glasses, why not trace around one of them instead so that your painted glass will match your real ones.

THE UNIQUE LANDSCAPE OF TUSCANY APPEARS TO HAVE BEEN LAID DOWN BY THE BRUSH OF A LOVING ARTIST—GENTLE UNDULATING HILLS CLAD WITH CYPRESS AND OLIVE TREES MEET THE REGIMENTAL LINES OF VINEYARDS, AND DISTANT BLUE HUES CONTRAST WITH SUN-SOAKED GOLDEN YELLOWS. THE PALETTE COULD NOT BE MORE PERFECT.

COLOR PALETTE

Chromium Oxide Green

Yellow Ochre

Burnt Sienna

Raw Sienna

Raw Umber

Red Oxide

Cobalt Blue

Payne's Grey

Medium Green latex (emulsion)

Pure White

But Tuscany may not, of course, be your preferred rustic setting—inspiration can be drawn from many different areas, such as the lavender fields of Provence, the olive groves of Spain, or corn fields of the American Mid-West. Whatever scene you decide on, composition is the most important aspect of this type of mural, with different trompe l'oeil elements leading the eye deeper into the picture. In this example, the glass of wine leads to the converging lines of the vineyard and then to the old monastery. The monastery and the cypress trees on the left then frame the distant hills and hamlets. Color is also used to suggest depth, with cool recessive blues and jade greens in the far distance, and more intense greens, browns, and yellows in the foreground.

CHOOSING A SITE

The Italians are renowned for their love of good food and fine wine, so an informal dining room or kitchen would make the perfect setting for this type of scene—ideal as a talking point during a meal, or to provide inspiration when tackling a new Italian recipe. The crumbling wall effect can be carried across all the walls to give the whole room a rustic feel.

FINDING VISUAL REFERENCE

To find inspiration for this scene, I looked through various travel brochures on the region for suitable images that could be put together to form the overall composition. I found a picture of an old monastery, one of a vineyard, and several references for distant hills and highlands showing the subtle colors and tonal gradations that suggest distance. Try not to copy photographic reference slavishly, or your design may become too rigid—just treat the visual references as rough pointers to content and color. If you are making a composite design from several images, remember that the light source will not be the same in all of them. In the example shown on these pages, the light comes from the left.

STEP
BY STEP

STEP 1 ▶ ▶ ▶

Plan out your window, using a level to draw in your vertical and horizontal lines. Remember that the position of your horizon will depend upon where your mural is most commonly viewed from, for example a seated or standing position, and will not always be in the center. The point at which the horizontal and vertical lines intersect is the vanishing point for the one-point perspective.

Attach a piece of string to the vanishing point, and with a charcoal pencil lightly draw in the diagonal depth lines—2–3 inches (5–7.5cm) should be sufficient—inside the window shape. Draw in the outside edge of the window using these diagonals.

The string can be used to plan louver windows as well. Refer to the Louver Doors element (pages 70–73) to plan the two windows and work out the foreshortened measurements. Don't worry about the inside details at this stage, as they will be tackled when the windows are blocked in. (See Tip, below.)

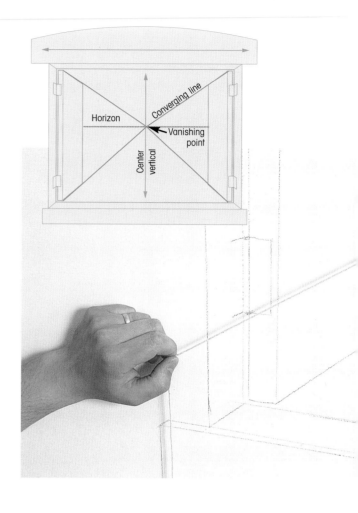

STEP 2 ◀ ◀ ◀

Loosely sketch a stone lintel above the window, wider than the window on each side by a few inches. The top of the lintel is slightly curved. Add a sill at the bottom of the window, also wider than the window. (See Stone Urn in Niche with Curtain, pages 90–95 for a similar example.)

Using a No. 3 round brush and Red Oxide mixed with a little water, paint in all the outlines. Use a straightedge such as a level to keep the lines true on the windows, but this is not strictly necessary for the surrounds. Smudge the line outward here and there to indicate chipping in the surface around the window.

TIP Before you remove the string and carry on to the next step, make a note of where the vanishing point is by measuring the distance to the top or bottom of the window. You will need to use the string and the vanishing point again later to plan the louvers, and it can be difficult trying to re-establish the original vanishing point after you have begun painting.

STEP 3 ▶ ▶ ▶

Fix a large sheet of semi-transparent transfer paper to the wall, and draw the horizon line over the top if you can't see it clearly. Have your visual references nearby so you can refer to them easily, then lightly sketch the landscape in graphite pencil using the horizon as a guide: the highlands and background will usually be above it, and the foreground below. Don't worry too much over details—a general suggestion of trees and foliage and the way the land rises will suffice. Use a level to ensure that the lines of the monastery are correct and that the cypress trees are not leaning. Transfer the image (pages 34–35), and, as before, paint the landscape outlines with Red Oxide.

STEP 4 ◀ ◀ ◀

Mix up a color wash using Yellow Ochre, Raw Umber, and Pure White mixed with about 15 parts water. This is the base color for the whole of the mural including the crumbling wall, so use a large decorator's brush to cover the entire area, brushing the paint in all directions and making sure you catch any runs. If you are carrying the effect along any other walls, paint these at the same time.

STEP 5 ▶ ▶ ▶

Mix up three or four shades of blue in plastic cups, using varying quantities of Cobalt Blue and Pure White with about one part water. Make a note of the contents of each pot on the side, for example Sky 1, Sky 2, etc. Using a ⅝-inch (16mm) flat brush and the darkest sky tone, begin painting the sky from the top downward, taking the color down the small gap in between the louver windows and the left- and right-hand window edges.

S T E P   6 ▶ ▶ ▶

Mix up two shades of blue for the distant hills, using Cobalt Blue and Pure White mixed with a little Burnt Sienna and one part water. These should be roughly the same tone as the two darker sky blues. Paint the hills using the ⅝-inch (16mm) flat brush and working from the top down. The light source is from the left, so I have used some of the lighter shade on this side and have let the color wash show through in places. Use the darker tone to suggest very distant foliage about halfway down the hills and to suggest variations in the land, but try not to get bogged down in detail in this area. Vague suggestions will enhance the illusion of distance and contrast with more detailed foreground elements.

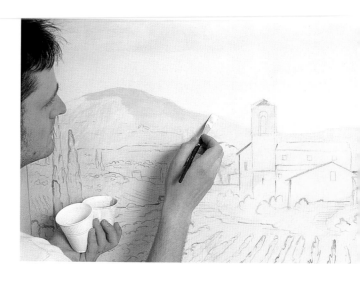

S T E P   7 ◀ ◀ ◀

Mix up two light shades of green using Chromium Oxide Green, Yellow Ochre, and some Pure White with about one part water. Using the ⅝-inch (16mm) flat brush and a No. 9 round brush, paint in all the trees, foliage, and vineyard, working freely and avoiding any detail. The whole picture is built up gradually and you will find yourself returning to certain areas and tweaking them slightly. This is why it is important to label your paint pots.

S T E P   8 ▶ ▶ ▶

Mix up two jade greens in plastic pots, using an equal amount of Cobalt Blue and Chromium Oxide Green, with Pure White and a little Yellow Ochre. Mix more white into one pot to make a lighter shade, and mix in one part water in each pot. With these two colors and the deeper blue used for the hills, paint some distant foliage and cypress trees with a No. 3 round brush. Again, avoid too much detail—one short brushstroke could represent a cypress tree in the distance. Use the blue for the most distant foliage, blending it into the jade greens as you progress down the landscape, smudging the paint with a finger in places. Make the land undulate slightly, with the gaps between the foliage giving the suggestion of distant fields. If the foliage starts to look too dark or defined, simply wash a little light blue over them to amend the color, using a ⅝-inch (16mm) flat brush dipped first in water.

STEP 9 ▶ ▶ ▶

In a plastic pot, mix up another green similar to those mixed in step 7, but with a little more Chromium Oxide Green. Use this color and the ⅝-inch (16mm) flat brush to begin deepening the trees and foliage in the middleground and foreground, stippling with the brush to give texture to the greenery. Bring in some of the lighter greens as well so that the foliage does not become too dark. Mix some Raw Umber, a little Yellow Ochre, and Pure White with one part water, and paint some shadows on the soil under the vineyard rows and the trees and foliage on the middleground, combining this color with the base color wash to blend in the shadows.

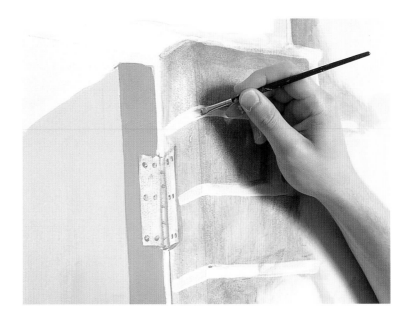

STEP 10 ◀ ◀ ◀

Using the same shadow color and a ¼-inch (6mm) flat brush, add some shadows and detailing to the monastery, noting the way in which shadows are cast by one part of the building onto another and how the line of shadow alters where the surface is at a different angle. For example, the shadow seems to enlarge on the roof of the monastery. Define the windows, making short vertical strokes with the same brush, and suggest windowsills with small lines beneath the windows. Take care with the lines of the arching at the top of the tower, as these create a perspective effect that gives depth to the building. Mix some of the shadow color into white to make a highlight color, and pick out the detailing where the light strikes.

STEP 11 ▶ ▶ ▶

Block in the louver shutters. With the window and landscape broadly established, it is a good time to plan the crumbling wall effect. (See Crumbling Wall, pages 58–63 for more detail). Use the shadow color from steps 9 and 10 to paint the outline, then block in the area with a paint wash consisting of Burnt Sienna, a little Raw Umber, and about six parts water. Use the shadow tone also to paint a cast shadow beneath and to the right of the windowsill and to add definition and cracks around the lintel. When adding mortar lines to the brickwork on the inside of the window opening, use the piece of string fixed at the vanishing point.

Paint into any cracks and chips around the edge of the window with the background color. Here I have just touched into a crack on the stone lintel with some of the deep sky-blue color. Around the window, the bricks jut out from the mortar, so paint out a tiny amount of mortar using the appropriate background color.

STEP 13 ▲▲▲

Now add some cloud to the sky using a ⅝-inch (16mm) flat brush and the light sky blue mixed with Pure White (see page 87, step 9). To add further color to the clouds, mix a wash of Pure White and Flesh Tint, and brush a little of this into some of the clouds and where the sky meets the hills, again using the flat brush.

STEP 14 ◀◀◀

With Chromium Oxide Green in one pot and the same color mixed with a little black in another, return to the trees and foliage middleground and foreground. Stipple the foliage, vineyard, and the olive tree next to the monastery with a ⅜-inch (10mm) flat brush, making the color deeper at the bottoms. Shape the cypress trees. Keep the right-hand side of each tree, which is in shadow, slightly deeper in tone.

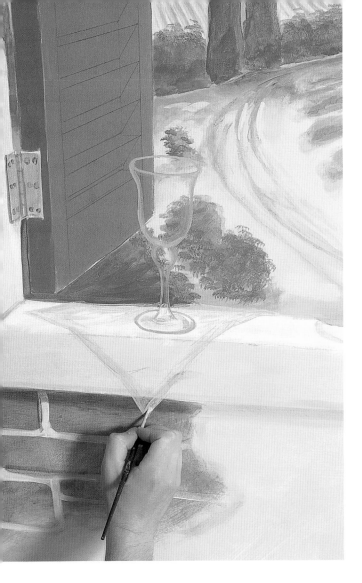

STEP 15 ◀◀◀

Draw a wine glass on transfer paper, remembering that it should be life size, and transfer the image to the wall. Beneath the wine glass, sketch in a napkin draped over the windowsill using a No. 1 round brush and the same blue that was used to paint the hills. Block it in using the ⅝-inch (16mm) flat brush. Make the color darker where the napkin hangs down in front of the windowsill and also around and inside the base of the glass. Carry the color up the glass stem a little, and paint in the outline of the glass using Payne's Grey mixed with a little Raw Umber and Pure White.

STEP 16 ▼▼▼

Block in the wine glass from the stem to two-thirds of the way up, using a ¼-inch (6mm) flat brush and Red Oxide diluted with a little water. To represent the surface of the wine, paint an ellipse slightly narrower than that at the rim of the glass; this top surface reflects light, and so will be lighter in color than the rest of the wine. Mix some Chromium Oxide Green into the Red Oxide to make a deeper tone. Gradually build up the shading from the edges of the glass and where the stem joins it to suggest curvature. Take a little of the Red Oxide and the darker tone down the stem a little to suggest the reflected colors.

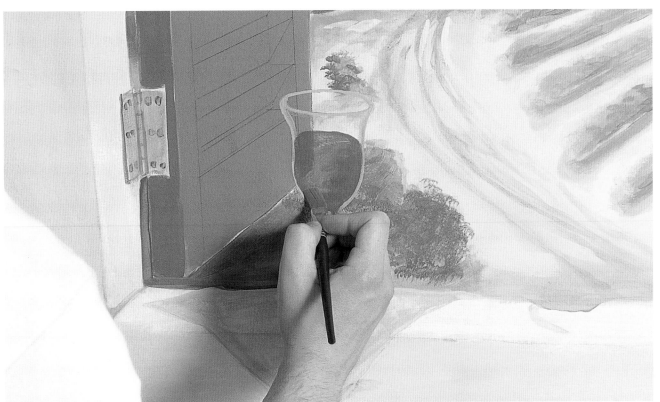

Now return to the louver windows and work out the placing of the slats using the technique shown in the Louver doors element (pages 70–73) and referring to the diagram on page 38. For the slats on the left-hand window, mix the base green and the deep green, and for those on the right-hand window mix the base green and the light green. Paint the glimpses of landscape between the slats with the small round brush. You only need a little detail to suggest the continuing foliage and background colors.

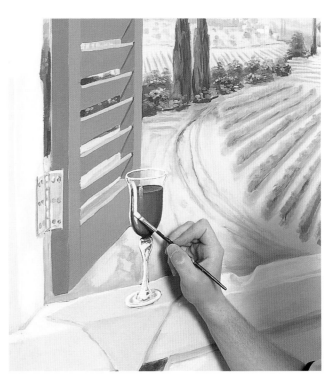

STEP 18 ▶▶▶

Add the final detailing and highlights to the wine glass, using the Payne's Grey, Raw Umber, and white mixture to suggest deep tones in the surface, especially down the stem and around the base. Add some fine darker blue shadows at the glass base, and paint touches of the background colors in areas where they would be seen through the glass. Here you can see the edge of the louver window and the sandy earth color at the top of the glass. Add a cast shadow beneath and to the right of the napkin under the windowsill.

STEP 19 ◀◀◀

Now add all the final detailing, such as the steps rising up to the monastery. These can be suggested by horizontal brushstrokes made with a No. 3 round brush and some Yellow Ochre mixed with Raw Umber and Pure White. Use two different shades to emphasize the steps, adding shadows where they meet the foliage. Highlights and lowlights on the trees and foliage can be added with either a ³⁄₈-inch (10mm) flat or a No. 3 round brush. (For more details, see Stone Archway & Classical Garden, pages 101–102, steps 10–12.) Add final details to the brickwork and wall (see Crumbling Wall, pages 60–62, steps 6–11). Finally, don't be afraid to do a little tweaking to any aspect of the mural even at this late stage.

VARIATIONS
LANDSCAPES
AND WINDOWS

VARIATION 1

Similar colors to those in
the Tuscany Window palette
have been used to produce
a very different landscape,
painted, appropriately, on
a Chinese wardrobe.

VARIATION 2

A field of bright lavender
adds a different element
to this rustic scene, and
repeats the purple of the
room's interior.

INDEX

Page numbers in *italics* refer
to illustrations/captions

CREDITS

Quarto would like to thank and acknowledge the following for supplying pictures reproduced in this book:

AKG Berlin: pages 8, 9 (above & below), 10, 11, 12 (above & below)
Mexicolore: page 13
Elizabeth Whiting Associates: pages 17 (below), 20, 21 (above)
Ward Design Group (mural painted by Christopher Westall): page 105 (above)
Davies Keeling & Trowbridge: page 105 (below)

All of the other trompe l'oeil murals featured in this book were painted by Christopher Westall.

The author would like to thank Marie-Claire Muir, Elizabeth Healey, Piers Spence, Paul Forrester, Colin Bowling, and Michelle Pickering for their help in producing this book.

The author's work can be viewed on his website at www.mural-design.com